MANAGING BUSINESS GROWTH:

Get a Grip on the Numbers that Count

numbers
101 for
SMALL BUSINESS

MANAGING BUSINESS GROWTH:
Get a Grip on the Numbers that Count

Angie Mohr, CA, CMA

Self-Counsel Press
(a division of)
International Self-Counsel Press Ltd.
USA   Canada

Self-Counsel Press acknowledges the financial support of the Government of Canada through the Book Publishing Industry Development Program (BPIDP) for our publishing activities.

Printed in Canada.

First edition: 2005

Library and Archives Canada Cataloguing in Publication

Mohr, Angie
    Managing business growth: Get a grip on the numbers that count/ Angie Mohr.

    (Self-counsel business series)
    ISBN 1-55180-581-2

1. Small business—Growth. 2. Small business—Management.
3. Business planning. I. Title. II. Series: Self-counsel business series.
    HD62.7.M64 2004   658.1′6   C2004-902694-1

Screen shot on page 44 from Quickbooks *by Intuit. Used with permission.*

Self-Counsel Press
(a division of)
International Self-Counsel Press Ltd.

1704 N. State Street	1481 Charlotte Road
Bellingham, WA 98225	North Vancouver, BC V7J 1H1
USA	Canada

Contents

1   The Successful Entrepreneur   1

Why Small Businesses Fail   1

Managing versus Doing   2

The Four Foundation Walls   2

    Entrepreneurial drive and vision   4

    Record keeping   4

    Financial management   5

    Planning and strategizing   6

2   The Life Cycle of a Business   9

The Three Stages of a Business   9

Infancy   11

Maturity   12

Decline   12

At What Stage of the Life Cycle Is Your Business?   13

How Can My Business Use This Information?   14

3   A Systems Approach   17

Anatomy of a Franchise   18

A Real-Life Example   18

Benefits of a Systems Approach   18

Your Business as a Machine 19

Becoming the Head Mechanic 19

4   Analyzing the Status Quo 23

Entrepreneurial Drive and Vision 23

Record Keeping 24

Financial Management 24

Planning and Strategizing 25

The Busy Entrepreneur 25

Defining Processes and Procedures 27

5   Growing Your Business 31

Your Business Goals 31

Profit 32

Freedom 33

Recognition 33

Peace of mind 33

Planning for Growth 33

Good versus Bad Growth 34

The Three Ways to Grow Your Business 35

Attracting new customers 35

Selling them more 36

Selling to them more often 37

Leverage Revisited 37

6   Getting a Handle on Your Revenues 41

How Many Customers Do You Have? 42

How Often Do Your Customers Come to See You? 43

What Do Your Customers Spend? 45

What Kind of Customers Do You Have? 46

Fire Away! 47

The Next Step 47

7   Your Strategy 51

Your Business's Vision Statement 51

The Mission Statement 53

Your Operational Plan 55

8 Testing Change   59

  Advertising   60

  Prices   61

  Environment   63

9 Your Product or Service   67

  Why Should Customers Buy from You?   67

    Competing on price   67

    Competing on value   68

  How Is Your Business Different?   69

  Selling a Product   70

  Up Selling   70

  Providing a Service   71

  Teaching Your Customers   73

10 Your Customer Interactions   75

  Telephone Interactions   75

  The Art of Closing the Deal   77

    Getting more people to call   77

    Increasing your conversion rate   78

  Using Scripts   81

  A Word about Screening Callers   82

  Tracking Conversion Rate Changes   83

11 Your Marketing and Promotions   85

  The Lifetime Value of a Customer   85

  Covering the Cost of the "Dry Holes"   87

  Customers Beget Customers   88

12 Your People   91

  How Do You Know When It's Time to Hire?   91

  What Will a New Employee Do?   92

  The Laws of the Land   93

  Attracting Quality Employees   95

  The Interview   97

  Hiring from an Employment Agency   98

Goal-Based Compensation 98
So Long, Farewell, Auf Wiedersehen, Adieu 99

13 Your Systems 103
The Goals of Systemization 103
"How We Do It Here" 104
Continuous Improvement 105

14 Business Acquisitions 109
Another Way to Grow 109
What Are You Buying? 110
    Asset purchase 111
    Share purchase 111
    Goodwill 111
    Customer lists 112
Valuing the Acquisition 112
    Floor price 114
    Ceiling price 114
Evaluating the Choices 115

15 Exit Strategies 117
Your Personal Goals 117
Heading for the Exits 118
    Passing on the business to your children 118
    Selling the business to an outside party 118
    Liquidating your business 119
What's My Business Worth? 119
Getting Ready for the Sale 120
The Mechanics of the Sale 121

16 What Happens Next? 123
A Last Word 124

Appendix 1 — Resources for the Growing Business 125
Online Resources 125
Must-Read Books for Entrepreneurs 126

Glossary 129

Diagrams

1 The Four Foundation Walls   3

2 The Life Cycle of a Business   10

3 Typical Time Chart for a Business Owner   25

4 Recommended Time Chart for a Business Owner   26

Samples

1 Customer Survey Form   43

2 Billings by Customer Report   44

3 Terminating a Customer   48

4 Vision Statements   52

5 Mission Statement   54

6 Telephone Interactions   76

7 Potential Customer Interaction Review Form   80

8 Telephone Script   82

9 Documenting Your Work Processes   94

10 Employment Advertisement   96

11 Human Resource Policy   106

12 Valuing a Business Acquisition   113

Checklists

1 The Successful Entrepreneur   7

2 The Life Cycle of a Business   15

3 A Systems Approach   21

4 Analyzing the Status Quo   29

5 Growing Your Business   40

6 Getting a Handle on Your Revenues   49

7 Your Strategy   57

8 Testing Change   65

9 Your Product or Service   74

10 Your Customer Interactions   84

11 Your Marketing and Promotions   89

12 Your People   101

13 Your Systems   108

14 Business Acquisitions   116

15 Exit Strategies   122

Notice to Readers

Laws are constantly changing. Every effort is made to keep this publication as current as possible. However, the author, the publisher, and the vendor of this book make no representation or warranties regarding the outcome or the use to which the information in this book is put and are not assuming any liability for any claims, losses, or damages arising out of the use of this book. The reader should not rely on the author or the publisher of this book for any professional advice. Please be sure that you have the most recent edition.

Acknowledgments

I would like to thank the following people and organizations for their assistance and support during the writing of this book:

Self-Counsel Press: Without the encouragement and expert guidance of my wonderful publishers, this series would not exist.

McClurkin Ahier and Company: For all of their support during the writing and touring process.

My family and friends. In particular, my husband, Jeff, and munchkins, Alex and Erika.

Introduction

Think of your business as a machine — one that needs monitoring, maintenance and the occasional rebuild. You, as the owner and manager of the business, are the head mechanic. It's your job to make sure the business is operating at its peak performance. It's easy for small-business owners to get mired in the day-to-day operations, but it's critical to remember why you're here: to oversee the business machine.

The benefits of taking this approach to your business are numerous. If your business runs efficiently, that means that it will run in your absence — while you're sleeping, on vacation, or spending time with your family. This allows you greater freedom than those business managers who can never leave their operations because their businesses are dependent on them to run. Those business owners see themselves as a part of the machine, rather than the head mechanic. They are chained to their businesses. Not only does that not give them freedom to get away for a while, it doesn't allow them to spend the necessary time strategizing and planning for the future of their business. They're too busy doing what the business does.

For example, if you own and manage a grocery store, your job as the head mechanic is to ensure that the business runs automatically and with the least amount of intervention on your part. This frees you to work on promotions, marketing, and financial strategizing. You will not need to be looking over the cashier's shoulder

CASE STUDY

Joe and Becky had come a long way in the past year. The husband and wife team own Joe's Plumbing, a small residential and commercial plumbing service that they started five years ago and still run out of their home.

Last year, their business situation reached the boiling point when Becky realized that she was snowed under with billings and administration, Joe was working all hours of the day and night, and they had no idea if they were making any money. It sure didn't feel that way to Becky as she was always juggling funds between their personal and business accounts and trying to figure out what bills had to be paid in which order and which ones could wait for a while.

They had grown out of their scrap-paper bookkeeping system and had no idea where to begin to fix the mess that they were in. Then they met Vivian, an experienced business accountant. Vivian listened carefully to Joe and Becky's concerns and then set up a plan for them to get back on track with the operational side of the business and to work on a more useful bookkeeping system. Vivian showed them how to budget expenses and forecast for the future. She taught them how to determine payback on capital expenditures, and how to deal with debt and their relationship with their bankers. Joe and Becky finally felt as if they were on solid ground for the first time in years. (To find out more about Joe and Becky's business adventures to date, please refer to the first and second books in the *Numbers 101 for Small Business* series, *Bookkeepers' Boot Camp* and *Financial Management 101*.)

ten hours a day to know whether your business is profitable. Rather, you will be able to review a management report to find out whether or not you are on track. This allows you to step in and correct any diversions from your business plan or to take advantage of sudden opportunities. If you are buried in the day-to-day operations of the business, you will likely miss these issues.

Managing Business Growth: Get a Grip on the Numbers that Count is the third book in the Self-Counsel Press *Numbers 101 for Small Business* series, aimed at small-business owners. In this book, we look at those critical processes that separate successful businesses from failures, and consider how to apply those financial processes to your business. We will cover many areas of managing your business, including strategizing, finances, operational management, and human resources. We will set up and monitor a strategic plan for your business, and learn how to test all your strategy changes to ensure that they are producing results.

How to Use This Book

Managing Business Growth walks you through the process of building a better business, one that runs efficiently and profitably. You don't need to read the chapters in sequence. Feel free to browse the table of contents and start with those chapters that interest you or apply to your business the most. I do, however, recommend that you eventually read the entire book, as each chapter has critical information to help your business. You may find that after reading this book, you not only look at your own business differently, but also the businesses that surround you every day: the coffee shop on the corner, the drycleaners, your child's daycare.

The concepts covered in *Managing Business Growth* are applicable regardless of the country or business climate in which you operate. The book is not written with specific tax laws or accounting rules in mind. Terminology may differ from country to country, and the dollar signs for some readers might be pounds or rupees or lire, but the underlying principles of the book are universally applicable.

We start by looking at why small businesses succeed or fail and then discuss the benefits of a systems approach to building your business machine. We then look at your strategy: what you want your business to accomplish in its lifetime. Chapters 8 through 13 cover specific areas of your business, including your product or service, your finances, your operations, your marketing, and your human resources. Chapters 14 through 16 look at more advanced areas of business management.

Managing Business Growth is written in an easy-to-digest manner that caters to busy entrepreneurs. It contains a blend of instruction and illustrated examples following the continuing story of Joe's Plumbing, a typical small business that is run by Joe and his wife, Becky. Joe and Becky face all the problems that most small-business owners face: how do they grow profitably, how do they know that their advertising is working, and how do they align their staff to their strategic goals?

The information in *Managing Business Growth* has been honed from the entrepreneurial workshops, radio broadcasts, and one-to-one training sessions I have developed in my accounting firm over the years.

You can find many downloadable tools and other useful information for small business owners at our website, <www.numbers101 .com>. Please surf by and download templates, screensavers, and other cool tools — and sign up for our free newsletter while you're there.

Managing Business Growth is the third book in the Self-Counsel Press *Numbers 101 for Small Business* series. If you want to brush up on your accounting basics, you may wish to read *Bookkeepers' Boot Camp,* the first book in the series. It covers the essentials of record keeping for small businesses and explains why it's necessary to track information. *Bookkeepers' Boot Camp* also teaches you how to sort through the masses of information and paperwork in your business, how to record what's important for your business, and how to use that information to grow your business for success.

If you need help with understanding what your financial statements are trying to tell you, you may wish to pick up *Financial Management 101,* the second book in the series. Here you will find clear, down-to-earth guidance to help you understand how to interpret your business's financial statements and how to use this information to create a more successful business.

CASE STUDY
continued

Now Joe and Becky are facing new challenges. They want to grow their business and hire another plumber to help Joe and an office assistant to help Becky. They also need to map out their strategy for Joe's Plumbing for the next several years. Joe wants to start looking at his life after Joe's Plumbing. He'd like to know how much the business would be worth if they were to sell it, and what the best way would be to plan for that. It's time to meet with Vivian again.

TI
Ei

Why Small Businesses Fail

As a resource to small-business owners, I've been a part of the business life of hundreds of companies. I've seen entrepreneurs take the seed of an idea and turn it into a multi-million dollar enterprise with dozens of employees. But, I've also seen entrepreneurs with that same great drive and vision fail — and fail miserably. What's the difference between these two types of entrepreneurs? How can two people with the same entrepreneurial spirit have such opposite outcomes?

My experience has shown me that successful business owners understand the importance of thinking about the business holistically. They don't just focus on their great idea, but they build a business from the ground up, taking care with every part of it.

They know they need a strong foundation for their business so they can build on it. With a strong foundation, they know they can expect their business to stay standing over the years. What makes a strong foundation when it comes to building a business? Successful owners know they need to build a broad base of skills in areas such as bookkeeping, financial management, and human resources. While those may not be the "sexiest" of activities, certainly not as exciting as choosing a logo or going public, they are critical to the success of the business.

CASE STUDY

Vivian set her coffee cup down on Becky's desk. Joe and Becky had set up an appointment with her to discuss the growth plans of Joe's Plumbing.

"So what made you decide that now, was the time to grow?" asked Vivian.

"Joe seems to work all the time now, and neither of us has enough time to devote to proper planning," Becky said. "We'd like to get the business to a point that it will almost run without us." She smiled at Joe. "Then maybe we can have a real vacation."

Joe chimed in. "And we've put into practice everything you've taught us. We have a real bookkeeping system now that lets us stay on top of our receivables and payables, and we know how to review our financial statements to figure out how we've done. Thanks to you, we even filed our taxes on time this year."

"You've done a great job getting a handle on your business up to this point," Vivian said. "But now, there are some things we must do before we start to grow the business. We need to have a look at the processes and procedures you have in place for your business and make sure that they are efficient and will handle the increase in business. Doing the planning upfront will save you immeasurable time down the road. Let's start with the basics."

Statistics abound when it comes to small-business failure in North America. Similar statistics exist in almost every country that harbors free enterprise. Here's one that will shock you: Over ten years, 96 percent of all small businesses fail. You read that correctly. For every 100 businesses started today, only four will still be around in ten years. What a horrible toll on people's lives!

That's the bad news. Here's the good news. According to a recent Dun and Bradstreet study, more than 85 percent of business failures are preventable. How? By better management, and in particular, better financial management. Despite what many people and the media will have you believe, it's not the competition or acts of God that sink these businesses. It's a lack of management skills and a poor foundation for the business. The good news is that these skills can be learned.

Managing versus Doing

Of all the challenges that entrepreneurs face when they start a small business, I see one critical problem time and time again. Many entrepreneurs lack the ability to differentiate between managing the business and doing what the business does.

For example, if you own and manage a variety store, then preparing budgets falls into the category of "managing the business," while waiting on customers is "doing what the business does."

It's easy to get caught up in the day-to-day workings of the business. Generally, most entrepreneurs are also managers, customer service representatives, human resource managers, and sales and marketing departments — and they probably have to clean the toilets too!

This problem is common in start-up companies. A hairdresser thinks that because he can cut hair, he can run a salon. A plumber opens up a plumbing business. Someone who makes a good cup of coffee thinks she can run a coffee shop. What these business owners don't realize is that management skill is a separate ability from the skill that it takes to do what the business does.

The Four Foundation Walls

There are four key management skills that every entrepreneur needs to succeed. You can look at them as the four walls that make up the foundation of a house. As you know, you can't properly build a house on a weak or badly formed foundation. Well, you may be able to get it built, but it won't last long.

Here's what it takes to succeed, whether your business is a sidewalk lemonade stand or Microsoft:

- Entrepreneurial drive and vision
- Record keeping
- Financial management
- Planning and strategizing

Take a look at Diagram 1.

Diagram 1
THE FOUR FOUNDATION WALLS

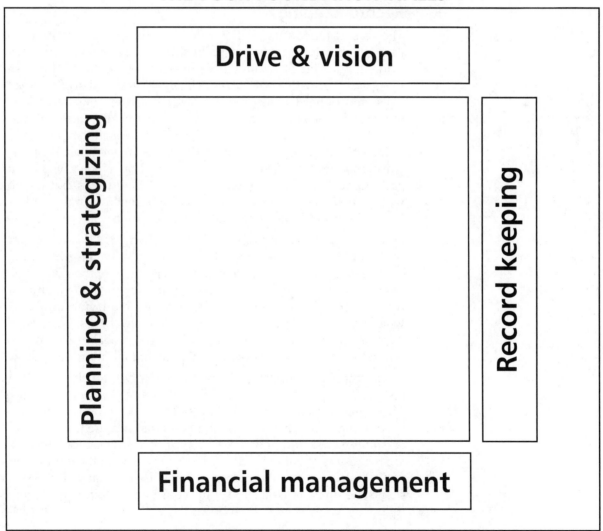

Entrepreneurial drive and vision

Every business starts with someone's vision. Vision is one of the main characteristics of an entrepreneur. An entrepreneur has the drive to build a business, with an image of what that business will look like down the road. He or she has the ability to think through a situation or look at a situation and see opportunity where many others would see nothing but problems. A true entrepreneur has confidence in himself or herself and a way of thinking that is unique. A real entrepreneur is born with these characteristics. You either have them or you don't, and they are impossible to teach. Without this first foundation wall, a successful enterprise is impossible.

Record keeping

The second foundation wall is record keeping. You have to keep track of the numbers for your business. Now, this seems self-evident, but time after time, I see business owners walk through my office door with a box (or more likely several boxes) of receipts, chits, and deposit books representing six, seven, or eight years' worth of financial records that they need magically turned into financial statements and tax returns. The only reason they're finally doing this is because the government has frozen their business bank accounts. Of course, as an accountant, I can always help them get caught up and get the government off their backs, but it's no way to run a business. They have no idea if they're winning or losing, never mind if they're actually making any money.

I sit down with each of these business owners. I fix their paper trail problems and talk about the need to get a better grip on the bookkeeping and ongoing financial management of their business. Often, sadly, it's too late by then, and they're living hand-to-mouth. They spend enormous amounts of time trying to decide what payments they can bounce so that the paychecks don't. They have neither the time nor money — or, most probably, the energy — left to set up a proper operational plan and monitor it regularly.

Recording your business's numbers involves much more than just setting up software such as *QuickBooks* or *Simply Accounting*. These programs don't actually do the record keeping for you. You need to plan out what information you must capture to run a successful business and how to best report that information. Recording the results of your operations is a critical wall in the foundation of the house you're building. Everything else rests on it, and if you spend the time necessary to set up your bookkeeping system the right way, you've created a solid wall.

What does it take to set up a proper bookkeeping system?

- **The right tools:** Every business is different. The method you use to collect the information you need should be based on the needs of your business, whether the solution is *QuickBooks* or an *Excel* spreadsheet or a manual ledger.

- **The right information:** What information is critical to know? Do you need to know which of your ten products is making the most money? Do you need to know how many hours you billed out this month? Then you need to set up your bookkeeping system to track this information for you.

- **The right output:** How are you going to look at this information? My experience has shown me that if you make your system too time intensive or elaborate, it breaks down. You should be able to get at the results with a few clicks of the mouse.

Setting up and maintaining a proper record keeping system is covered in the first book of the *Numbers 101 for Small Business* series, *Bookkeepers' Boot Camp*.

Financial management

The third foundation wall is financial management: understanding what the numbers are telling you. It's no use having your sales figures broken down 700 different ways if you can't tell whether or not you made money last year, or if you can't tell if one part of your operation is needlessly draining cash from the whole business.

You can't really know how you are doing and which way to go next without a basic understanding of your business numbers. Even businesses that have been around for a decade or more can struggle with this concept. Their owners and managers either can't or won't read their financial statements. So many financial disasters can be uncovered early through proper analysis. And like any disease of the body, early detection usually lowers the death rate. A wise entrepreneur can diagnose many impending business disasters and start treatment early to prevent further bleeding.

Financial management means taking all the figures you've tracked and testing them against some benchmarks. Ask yourself: Do you know what financial ratios are? If you do, are you familiar with the key financial ratios for your business? Do you have any idea what your break-even or capacity levels are? These are important markers for your business. They can tell you about profit, liquidity, and solvency. They can tell you if you have too much exposure to debt or too little. They can tell you if you have enough money in the short term and the long term.

Think of these benchmark tests as laboratory tests that a doctor would order if you weren't feeling well. Through laboratory analysis of your blood, you'd learn if your potassium levels are too high, for example. The doctor would compare your results to benchmarks in order to assess whether or not your levels are normal. Once you have learned to read your financial information, financial analysis can tell you whether your business is operating at a normal level or if there is some underlying disease. And, like many diseases of the body, it's important to catch the symptoms of your business's disease early before the situation becomes terminal.

Financial Management 101, the second book in the *Numbers 101 for Small Business* series, teaches you how to interpret the story that your numbers are telling you.

Planning and strategizing

The final foundation wall of your business is planning and strategizing, which is different from entrepreneurial vision, although it may sound similar at first. Planning and strategizing takes your business's historical performance and projects it into the future. It helps you understand the impact of both internal and external forces on your future financial performance and allows you to take steps to make any necessary changes.

For example, a business can be seemingly running along just fine, oblivious to its financial position. There always seems to be enough money in the bank to cover expenses, and the income statement that prints off almost automatically every month from the software program tells the owner that there is indeed net income. Then the business decides to have a big promotion; they will provide three hours of free technical support for every computer they sell.

They buy 600 units from their supplier, for which they have 30-day terms (i.e., they have to pay the supplier in 30 days). The promotion starts the next week and runs for two weeks. Every customer gets 30 days to pay. The problem is that the business will need to pay its supplier before the money comes in from the customers, which can lead to a serious cash flow issue. And it all could have been prevented by projecting cash needs into the future and strategizing.

In this book, we'll examine the issues of effectively planning and strategizing for your business.

Checklist 1
THE SUCCESSFUL ENTREPRENEUR

1. I have spent time mapping out the long-term direction of my business. ❑

2. I know my strengths and weaknesses as an entrepreneur. ❑

3. For those skills in which I am the weakest, I have formulated a plan to learn the necessary information. ❑

4. I have a record-keeping system for my company that gives me accurate and timely information. ❑

5. I have determined the critical revenue and expense breakdowns that will help me to manage my business strategically. ❑

6. I have calculated my break-even and capacity points for my business. ❑

7. I know what the key financial ratios are for my particular business. ❑

8. I know how to read my financial statements and understand the story they are telling me. ❑

9. I have prepared cash flow projections for my business for the next five years. ❑

10. I have carved out at least 20 percent of my time for planning and strategizing activities. ❑

The Life Cycle of a Business

It may be difficult for you to think of any business, especially your own, as having a fixed life span. You probably would like to think that your business will outlive you and your children and grandchildren — that it will still be around 500 years from now. But, in reality, that is not likely.

It's almost impossible to determine how long your business will last. Some companies have survived generations, although these too will someday cease to exist. Japan's Hoshi Hotel has been around since 718 AD, surviving almost 50 generations of the Hoshi family. Barovier & Toso has been making glass in Venice since 1295. The oldest existing family firm in the United Kingdom, John Brooke & Sons, Ltd., has been in operation since 1541. In North America, the Hudson's Bay Company first started fur trading in 1670. Each of these companies has experienced ups and downs over their long and venerable existence, but they have still followed the same life cycle that your business will experience.

The Three Stages of a Business

Every business goes through a natural evolution over its lifetime. The only difference between businesses is how quickly they progress through the cycles.

The natural life cycle of any business can be broken into three stages: infancy, maturity, and decline (see Diagram 2). Each of the stages has unique identifiers. A business in the infancy stage, for example, will have operational characteristics and trends that are very different from a business in the decline stage.

Let's look at each stage in more detail.

Diagram 2
THE LIFE CYCLE OF A BUSINESS

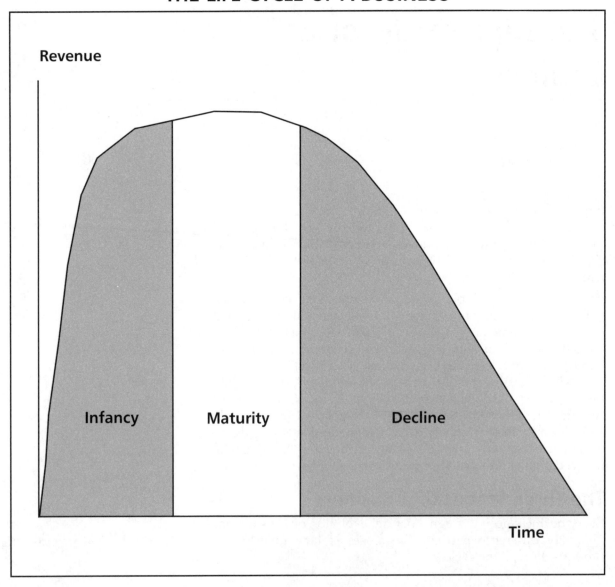

Infancy

Infancy is where every new business starts out. It is a time signified by negative cash flows, rapid growth, and capacity bottlenecks.

Businesses that are just beginning their operations often find that their outflows of cash are greater than their inflows. If you start your business from scratch, you must build up your customer base before you have revenue. However, fixed expenses like rent, office staff, and insurance have to be paid whether you have no customers or 1,000 customers. The negative cash flow this creates is usually temporarily fixed by either owner investment or bank financing.

In general, businesses that are very capital intensive (e.g., those that require significant specialized equipment) have a greater negative cash flow at the beginning of their life cycle. Once revenues are high enough to cover both the direct cost of the product or service being sold and the overhead costs, then they begin to make profits. (For a fuller discussion of fixed cost behavior, refer the second book of the *Numbers 101 for Small Business* series, *Financial Management 101.*)

Businesses in the start-up phase tend to have quite dramatic revenue growth, which is easy to understand when you consider that when you grow from having no customers to one customer, you have increased revenues by 100 percent! If the business is filling a market niche, customers will either come over from other suppliers or will realize the need for the product or service, perhaps for the first time. Your customer base will continue to grow until the market need has been filled (i.e., all the potential customers have already come over). At this point, your business begins to move into the maturity phase.

Another frequent characteristic of infancy is that the business regularly hits its capacity. For example, a manufacturer will run his or her current equipment to its maximum capacity before he or she purchases a new one. A service provider will have his or her staff working overtime before hiring new staff.

Most of the consideration here is financial and relates back to the negative cash flows that we talked about earlier. If you don't have the money for new equipment, you will nurse your old equipment along for as long as you can. Another reason that capacity is often reached, though, relates to the ability (or inability) of the new entrepreneur to accurately predict demand for the product or service. If that demand and its related sales are underestimated, a business can be left scrambling to get orders filled quickly. Once a business has a longer history, and its manager has a better understanding of the industry and its trends, capacity issues become less pronounced.

When a business better understands its markets and customers and has absorbed most of the excess market demand in its industry, it will begin to shift into the maturity stage.

Maturity

In the maturity phase, a business has found its place in its industry and can more accurately predict its revenues and expenses.

The maturity phase is denoted by stable revenue growth (perhaps 5 percent to 10 percent per year) and positive cash flows. Mature businesses provide a consistent return to their investors and a stable salary to their managers.

Businesses stay in the maturity phase until they begin to decline, either through obsolescence or changes in the external market.

It is in the maturity phase that a business must begin to plan for its own demise (much like an individual should engage in retirement and estate planning well before those events take place). In Chapter 15, we will discuss exit strategies for a business in the maturity phase.

Decline

Every business eventually begins to slow down. Revenues begin to taper off and cash flow once again becomes a problem.

Why do once-healthy businesses die? Frequently, it's because the services or products that the business sells are no longer needed in the market place. Consumer tastes change or technology has advanced so that new products take the place of old ones. Forward-thinking businesses can stave off this decline, at least in the short term, by changing with the times and offering new products or services. Eventually, however, new players will enter the field and will erode market share.

Businesses have differing responses to going into the "golden years" of their existence. If a business is not planning and strategizing appropriately, it may not even realize it is in decline. The business can struggle along for several years in this phase (at least until the money runs out) and not understand why revenues are declining and cash flow is tight.

Other businesses put themselves up for sale, realizing that they still have solid components that a newer business may want to integrate into their operations. Some businesses choose to wind up operations and the investors find other avenues of investment.

At What Stage of the Life Cycle Is Your Business?

By using the signposts and discussion above, you should be able to figure out where your business fits into the life cycle model. Is it a new business, with leaping revenues and no cash? Or is it more stable, with a predictable market demand?

It's important to know at what stage your business is in its life cycle, because it will help you in a myriad of ways, especially in the planning and strategizing area.

A real-life example of a company that understood its own vulnerability to obsolescence is the Minnesota Mining & Manufacturing Company. The name of this company may not be familiar to you but I'm sure you have heard of 3M, which is the name the company adopted as they changed their products over the years.

3M was born in 1902 in Two Harbors, Minnesota. Five investors started the company in order to mine a mineral deposit for grinding-wheel abrasives. This didn't work out because the deposit was found to have little value. The company began to focus on sandpaper products. Business was difficult in the start-up years and the company struggled until it could find more investors and develop new products.

In 1925, one of the laboratory assistants invented masking tape and a whole new line of products was born. 3M created Scotch tape, Scotchlite Reflective Sheeting for highway markings, and magnetic sound-recording tape. They invented dozens of products that we now would have a difficult time living without, including some that were originally intended for wartime use. In the 1970s and 1980s, 3M expanded into pharmaceuticals, radiology, energy control, and the office market (Post-It Notes being the major invention in this area).

3M is now a multinational corporation with revenues of over US$15 billion a year. The company reports that approximately 30 percent of these sales come from products created in the past four years. 3M understood that its strength was creating new products for emerging markets using its core technologies. Had this company stuck to its original mandate of mining or even of selling sandpaper, it would not be around today. 3M has not hit decline yet as it has always managed to adapt to current market conditions. You must also do this in your small business if it is to survive.

How Can My Business Use this Information?

Knowing your business's place in the life cycle indicates a lot about what to expect in the coming years.

For example, if you have been in business for three years and have had revenue growth of 92 percent the first year, 76 percent the second year, and 14 percent the third year, you may be entering the maturity phase. Therefore, it would be ridiculous to predict 75 percent revenue growth in the fourth year. As Diagram 2 shows, in the maturity phase, revenue growth begins to slow as it climbs towards the top of the arch. It would probably make more sense to predict 8 percent to 10 percent growth in the fourth year.

If you have noticed a decline in revenues, triggering a more problematic cash flow, your business may be starting to decline. It's important to examine the underlying causes of the decline. Are there new products on the market? Do you have a customer service issue (i.e., can someone else do what you do faster, with better guarantees or fewer hassles)? You can only devise a response to the decline if you understand the cause.

Checklist 2
THE LIFE CYCLE OF A BUSINESS

1. I know which life cycle stage my business is in. ❑

2. I have projected my business's growth rate using the life cycle information. ❑

3. I have planned how to prolong the maturity phase of my business. ❑

4. I have analyzed the demand for my business's product or service and am comfortable that I can meet my customers' expectations. ❑

5. I have analyzed the external market conditions that affect my business and I understand the trends that will impact my business's future revenues. ❑

6. I have considered new products or services that I can offer in order to continue my company's growth. ❑

7. I have reviewed the opportunities to purchase and integrate another business into my own to strengthen market demand. ❑

A Systems Approach

What would you say if I told you that your small business has a lot in common with McDonald's or FedEx? You may wonder at first what, if anything, your small business has to do with these franchises. They are giants in their respective industries and employ thousands of people. Your business, on the other hand, is made up of you and perhaps a handful of staff.

But these large franchises were once small, too. They started with one person's dream of how a business should operate. Those entrepreneurs experimented with their business models time and time again until they got it right.

What successful franchises have done exceedingly well is to build and monitor systems in their procedures.

At McDonald's, for example, there is a system for greeting the customer, a system for preparing the food, and a system for cleaning the bathrooms. These and a myriad of other systems allow you, the customer, to have a consistent experience every time you visit. Neither the president of McDonald's nor the restaurant manager needs to be there to make sure you're properly looked after.

Are you able to say the same thing about your business? Or do you feel that you need to be there every minute to make sure that nothing disastrous happens?

Let's take a look at how franchises work and the systems they use. Then we can begin designing your business to operate in a similarly effective manner.

"One of the reasons you both are feeling so overwhelmed," Vivian said, "is that you both *are* the business."

Joe looked puzzled. "I'm not sure what you mean by that. Of course, we are the business. There's no one else."

Vivian smiled. "But there will never be anyone else until you begin to systematize your business."

"Oh, I think I understand," Becky said. "You mean we have to write down how we do things, kind of like an operations manual."

"Well, I do mean that," Vivian said, "but it's more than that too. You need to start looking at your business and personal goals to make sure that your growth plan will fit in with them. Then you will have to make sure that each of your processes and procedures gets you to your goal. If you just start growing without doing this legwork first, it's like turning on a fire hose full blast without controlling the stream of water. It will be all over the place."

Joe frowned. "And then we'd be working even more."

Anatomy of a Franchise

You may not consciously think about this when you walk into your favorite Dunkin' Donuts to pick up your daily honey dip or when you pull into Midas Muffler to get your seasonal lube, oil, and filter, but from the moment you enter the door, you have witnessed a process. If you walk into these businesses tomorrow or the day after that, you will have a practically identical experience. And that is the strength of a franchise. Customers know exactly what to expect. They know that they will be greeted in the same manner, that the product or service will be the same quality every time, and any customer issue will be handled in the same way.

A Real-Life Example

Let's have a look at a real franchise. Geeks On call® is a company that provides on-site computer services to residential and commercial customers. Geeks is a franchise. The head office sells the exclusive rights to franchisees to operate in a certain territory. It also provides ongoing support and assistance to the franchisees to help them operate their businesses in a consistent and profitable manner according to the Geeks strategy.

To become a Geeks franchisee, you must pay a franchise fee upfront, and then ongoing fees, to the head office for advertising. You also pay them a royalty of a certain percentage of your sales. In return, you reap the benefits of the Geeks advertising campaigns and ongoing technical and sales support.

Do you have to be a computer programmer to run a Geeks franchise? Absolutely not (although many are). The main criteria are entrepreneurial drive and vision. You can hire the computer technicians to work for you. This is the benefit of a systems approach — the systems and expertise have already been developed and, as long as you follow the systems, you will be a successful business owner. It's the same reason that you do not need to be a chef (or even be able to boil water) to become a McDonald's franchisee.

Benefits of a Systems Approach

The benefits of taking what franchises do well and applying those concepts to your own business are many. How would you feel if every time you walked into your favorite Dunkin' Donuts, the experience was different? Now put yourself in your customers' shoes. Do you want them to have the same comfort level when dealing with you, always knowing what to expect? Of course you do! It will not only set you apart from your competitors in your customers' eyes, but it will also make the operation of the business much more effective and enjoyable for you.

Another often-overlooked benefit of taking a systems approach to your business is that, when you are ready to sell your business, you will have created a much more valuable business and will generally receive a higher price. Why is that? Think about it from the buyer's perspective. The buyer is purchasing a business that is practically "turnkey," meaning that they can walk in and, from day one, run the business exactly the same way that you did. They are buying the systems: the procedures and operations manuals that will ensure that they will be as successful as you have been.

Your Business as a Machine

Looking at your business as if it were a machine with cogs and wheels may be a new perspective for you. The more you see your business as a tangible thing, however, the more you will be able to envision what needs to be done to make it as effective and efficient as possible. You will need to make the fundamental paradigm shift from "I make money for myself" to "my business makes money for me." Although that may seem like a small change in wording, it represents a huge change in thinking — one that will make your business successful.

Becoming the Head Mechanic

Once you have made the shift to "my business makes money for me," your role in the business becomes clearer. Your main role is not to do what the business does (e.g., make bagels, cut hair, design buildings), although you may still function in that capacity. Your main role is to increase the operating efficiency of the business machine. You will ensure that all employees are following the systems that you have put in place and are performing consistently.

Becoming the head mechanic means that you will not be buried in the minutia of the business for 12 hours a day, but will truly be in a management role, helping your employees to be a part of the machine.

As head mechanic, your main tasks will be —

- Ensuring compliance with the systems
- Reviewing the impact the systems are having on the financial health of the business

CASE STUDY

"I don't think we've ever stopped to look at what we want out of this business," Becky said.

"And I've never thought about when I would want to retire," said Joe. "But it would actually be comforting to know where we're headed and how we're going to get there." He turned to Vivian. "So, what's the first step?"

"Let's have a look at the way you're doing things now," said Vivian, pulling out a pad of paper from her briefcase.

- Constantly testing the effectiveness of existing systems and altering them as required
- Building new systems as the business grows

Once you understand your true role in your business, you will find that you spend less time managing and have created more time for planning and strategizing.

Checklist 3
A SYSTEMS APPROACH

1   I have considered the benefits of systematizing my business.   ☐

2. I have taken notice of franchises that I deal with frequently
    and understand their systems.   ☐

3. I understand that my main function in my business is
    to manage and grow it; not just work in it.   ☐

4. I have mapped out my major management functions
    in my business.   ☐

5. I have analyzed my business from my customers' perspective.   ☐

6. I have put a plan in place that allows me to spend at least
    20 percent of my time on planning and strategizing activities.   ☐

Analyzing the Status Quo

Before we can look at growing your business soundly, we need to make sure that the foundation walls of your business's house have been solidly built. In Chapter 1, we looked at the four foundation walls of your business:

- Entrepreneurial drive and vision
- Record keeping
- Financial management
- Planning and strategizing

Let's take a more detailed look at each of these areas and make sure that your business is sound.

Entrepreneurial Drive and Vision

This is all about you and the vision that you have for your business. Remember back to when your business was nothing but an insistent thought in your head. You may have been working for someone else or raising your children or finishing school, but you knew what you wanted to do and how it should look.

That vision and drive to create a business should still be there now. In other words, the first criterion for *growing* a business successfully is the same as for *starting* one: the force of will and the creativity to create something spectacular.

Take some time and make sure that the spark is still there. If, for example, you currently feel burned out and overwhelmed by

CASE STUDY

the day-to-day operations of the business, you will need some time to regenerate yourself before you can put your efforts and talents into growing your business. Once you have made sure that your fundamental drive is still there, then it's time to examine the other three foundation walls.

Record Keeping

Okay, discussing bookkeeping is not the most exciting thing in the world, but, as you know by now, it is critical.

Examine your record keeping practices. Here's a quick checklist for you:

- Is your bookkeeping up to date?
- Are all supplier payments and government remittances being paid on time?
- Is your bookkeeping system giving you the information you need on a timely basis?
- Has your business outgrown your bookkeeping system?
- Are you doing your own bookkeeping when your time and talent would be better spent on managing or growing your business?

If you need a refresher on bookkeeping systems or hiring a bookkeeper, you may wish to refer back to the first book in the *Numbers 101 for Small Business* series, *Bookkeepers' Boot Camp*.

Financial Management

Once you have determined that your record keeping system is still optimal for your business, it's time to look at your financial management practices:

- Do you have an adequate system for preparing and analyzing budgets?
- Are you actively managing your business's key performance indicators?
- Do you have systems in place to track your accounts receivable and accounts payable?
- Do you have a handle on all the risks associated with your business, such as debt exposure, economic dependence, and foreign exchange risk?

If you need a refresher on financial management for your business, you may wish to refer to the second book in the *Numbers 101 for Small Business* series, *Financial Management 101.*

Planning and Strategizing

This is the foundation wall that we will spend the most time discussing in the remainder of this book. Planning and strategizing requires taking all our knowledge of our business's historical performance and projecting it into the future. It encompasses revenue and customer base growth, as well as resource and materials planning. It involves asking questions such as: How much capital will we need 12 months from now? How many people will we be hiring? If we spend $4,000 on advertising, what will that do to revenues?

The Busy Entrepreneur

As both the owner and manager (and perhaps salesperson, office clerk, bookkeeper, and toilet cleaner) of your business, the demands on your time are many. You may feel unsure how to appropriately apportion your time. It is natural for you to spend your time on the more immediate concerns, such as bookkeeping, talking to customers, and sales, rather than planning and strategizing. A typical split of an owner/manager's time might look like Diagram 3.

Diagram 3
TYPICAL TIME CHART FOR A BUSINESS OWNER

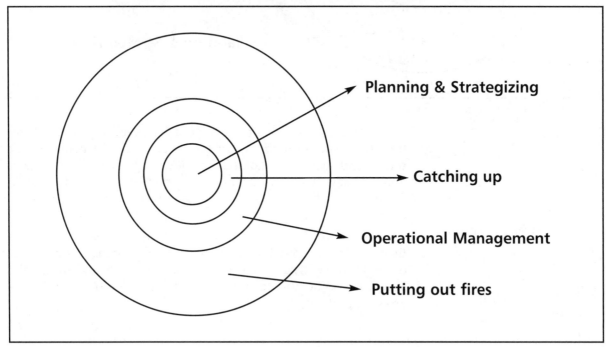

- Planning & Strategizing
- Catching up
- Operational Management
- Putting out fires

As you can see, this entrepreneur only spends whatever time he or she feels is left over for planning and strategizing. Because the more immediate work tends to expand to fill available time, there is frequently no time left over for proper planning.

A more appropriate split of time is shown in Diagram 4.

Diagram 4
RECOMMENDED TIME CHART FOR A BUSINESS OWNER

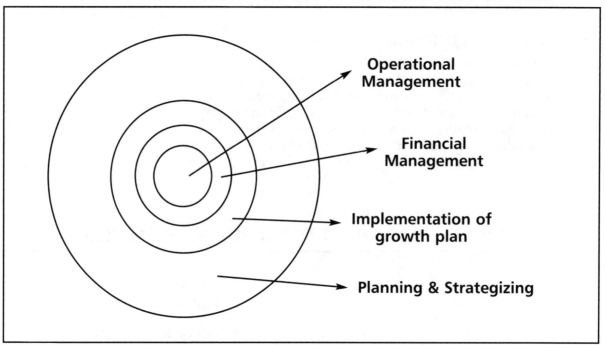

Operational
Management

Financial
Management

Implementation of
growth plan

Planning & Strategizing

As you can see, this entrepreneur has freed up much of the time he or she formerly spent on operational and management duties, and spends most of the time now on growing the business. You may say, "Well, that's all well and good, but I can't magically create time or hire a bunch of people to take over my operational duties."

The answer is systems. Once you have systems in place, the time required for the day-to-day management of the business will decrease. You will run the business more efficiently and effectively. You will also be able to spend your time where it counts — on growing profitably!

Defining Processes and Procedures

So, how do we start building systems into our growth model? We start by studying the processes we already have in place.

Write down all the processes in your business that you can think of. A process is any group of procedures that accomplishes a business goal. For example, some typical business processes might be:

- Handling telephone inquiries
- Making service calls to customers
- Billing procedures
- Accounts payable
- Cleaning the office
- Managing the inventory

You'll notice right off that some of these processes are internal and some are external. Internal processes are ones that the business must perform as part of its operations, but which are not visible to the customer or client. External processes are those that directly affect the customer or client. So, for example, the way the telephone is answered can have a direct impact on whether someone becomes a new customer, whereas how the bathrooms are cleaned does not have such a direct link (although dirty bathrooms ultimately can influence a customer's decision to go elsewhere).

Once you have identified as many processes as possible, take each one and break it down into its component procedures. For example, let's start with handling telephone inquiries. A breakdown of individual procedures might look like this:

Handling telephone inquiries

1. Telephone is answered by whomever is available (Employee #1).
2. Caller is greeted pleasantly using the company name.
3. Inquiry is answered if Employee #1 knows the answer, otherwise takes a message.
4. If message taken, it is written on a piece of paper and put on the desk of the person that the employee thinks can most likely answer the question (Employee #2).
5. Message is handled by Employee #2 if he or she knows the answer, otherwise, message paper is passed to another employee (Employee #3).

CASE STUDY

"Wow. It's hard to believe that we do so many different things — and we're just a small business. Can you imagine what Microsoft would have to document?" Becky said, flipping through Vivian's notebook.

Vivian smiled. "A company like Microsoft would go through this same process of documenting, fine tuning, and re-documenting. Although it would certainly be on a much larger scale."

Joe said, "One thing I noticed as we went through this exercise is that we don't always do things the same way. I'm sure that might affect how we grow the business, especially when it comes to following up on calls from potential customers. It looks like we have a lot of work to do in that area."

"There is lots to do but we've made a great start today by looking at the way you do things now. It will help us to identify weak areas as we go through the systematization process."

Chapter Summary

➡ Before you can grow your business profitably, it's critical to ensure that you have your four foundation walls in place: entrepreneurial drive and vision still intact, an appropriate record keeping system, ongoing financial management, and preliminary planning and strategizing.

➡ Most of your time is probably spent on the operational side of your business, but once you have systems in place, more time will be freed up for planning and strategizing.

➡ Start the business growth process with documenting your current processes and procedures.

These procedures make up the process of handling telephone inquiries. Now take each process in your business and document these procedures. Processes that you have forgotten will most likely present themselves to you at this time and you can add them to the list.

Note that we do not want to begin fleshing out the documentation for these processes at this time. We will be fine-tuning and in some cases getting rid of inefficient procedures and processes in the following chapters. Only once we have our new set of processes will we begin creating documentation for the processes in the form of a systems manual.

Checklist 4
ANALYZING THE STATUS QUO

1. I have re-examined my original intentions for starting my business. ❑

2. My bookkeeping is up-to-date and accurate. ❑

3. I have re-evaluated whether or not I need to hire a bookkeeper. ❑

4. I have an up-to-date budget for the current fiscal year. ❑

5. I have set up a management operating plan and am tracking my key financial indicators regularly. ❑

6. I have outlined all of my business's current processes for both internal and external functions. ❑

7. I have broken down all of my business processes into their individual procedures. ❑

Growing Your Business

In this chapter, we will begin to look at how to profitably grow your business. Many small businesses look only at getting new people in the door when they think about growing their business. In trying to attract these new customers, they take the "splatter gun" approach: placing ads and running marketing campaigns based on "gut feel" and pricing. They have no idea if these programs are working or if they are sending good money after bad down the sinkhole.

Growing your business takes more planning, testing, and discipline than that, however. In order to create a proper plan for growth, you must start by looking at what your goals are for your business.

Your Business Goals

When you first started your business, what did you envision five or ten years down the road? A huge corporation with dozens or perhaps hundreds of employees, and you sitting in the glass-walled corner office with its own fireplace and bar? Or did you have something smaller in mind, just you and a desk in your basement with the ability to run upstairs and put in a load of laundry occasionally?

Regardless of what stage your business is at, if you're contemplating growth, it's time to revisit your goals, both business and personal.

CASE STUDY

Many of these goals will be outlined in your business plan, which should be a living, breathing embodiment of your business and its projected future. (What, you don't have a business plan? Go and sit in the corner! Better yet, go back and read the second book in the *Numbers 101 for Small Business* series, *Financial Management 101,* for a discussion of financial measures and tracking systems.)

You may find that some of your goals conflict with one another. For example, you may want to pursue aggressive growth, which may entail lots of hands-on time. That will cause some challenges if another of your business goals is to spend more time with your family.

Let's take a look at some typical goals many entrepreneurs have, as well as some things for you to think about as you decide which business and personal goals are important to you.

Profit

The most common of small business goals is making money. How can you determine how much profit is reasonable to plan for? Start by looking at other businesses in your industry. It may be difficult to determine exactly what their profit position is (they're most likely private companies with confidential financial information), but with some experience you should be able to make a reasonable guess.

Start with what you know of their expenses. You should have a good handle by now on your own expenses and will therefore be able to ascertain what your competitors' cost structures must look like. Then, try to get a handle on their revenues. How many customers would you estimate they have? What does their pricing structure look like? These will provide a rough estimate of their profit. If those businesses have been in business longer than you have and are mature businesses, that level of profit is most likely reasonably attainable for your business as well.

Next, start thinking about your own profit goals. What do you need in the way of an ongoing income, either as a manager's salary or an investor's return on investment, to cover your living expenses and live comfortably? What do you want to put away into savings? Do you want to sell the business and retire early? This is where your personal and business financial goals merge. For example, if you are running a part-time T-shirt-making business out of your garage and your personal wealth goal is to become a millionaire by the age of 40, you may have to rethink one of those priorities.

Freedom

Freedom is another common entrepreneurial goal: Freedom from financial worry, freedom from bosses, freedom to set your own hours, freedom to write your own destiny. There are many types of freedoms you may think about when first starting your business. The tragedy is that many small-business owners don't plan effectively enough to ever experience those freedoms. They end up chained to their businesses, chasing after the first goal: profit.

Think about what's really important to you in the way of work-family balance. Do you want to work 20 or 60 hours per week? Do you want to be able to arrange your own work hours and not be chained to a retail location? Do you want to work as hard as possible for the first five years to get the business off the ground and then slow down? These are some important considerations when starting to develop your growth plan.

Recognition

Some entrepreneurs want to be recognized and respected — in their communities, in their industries, in their fields of expertise. You may want to be known as the leading expert in oriental rug cleaning, and your rug cleaning business is your platform from which to showcase that expertise. Take some time to consider if recognition is important to you.

Peace of mind

It may comfort you to know that you do not have to rely on anyone else for your source of income. You are creating your own wealth. This removes some of the risk that employees have of being completely dependent on an employer to get a paycheck. If this goal is important to you, it will be critical as you plan your business's growth to make sure that you recognize the more hidden sources of risk in a small business, and that you take steps to avoid them.

Planning for Growth

Now that you've looked at those business and personal goals that are important to you, it's time to begin your growth plan.

Some of this plan should already be embedded in your overall business plan. At the very least, you should have a 12-month and 5-year revenue and cash flow projection. You may also have a marketing and promotion strategy. What we are going to do now is to take that high-level planning and bring it down to street level, planning it piece by piece, testing its effectiveness, and putting numbers to it.

The revenue growth in your business plan may look something like this:

Year:	2005	2006	2007	2008	2009
Revenue:	$175,000	$218,750	$262,500	$301,875	$ 332,063
Growth:		25%	20%	15%	10%

This growth pattern would be typical of a business that will move from the infancy stage to the maturity stage in its life cycle during this five-year period. (See Chapter 2 for a discussion of a business's life cycle.)

We need to plan exactly how to achieve those levels of revenues. It's not enough to simply place some newspaper ads and cross our fingers. We must have a step-by-step strategy. But first, let's make sure we understand the difference between good growth and bad growth.

Good versus Bad Growth

Growth is growth, you say? Take it and run! This strategy has bankrupted many small businesses. It's critical to understand why and to be able to divert yourself from that path if you find yourself starting to meander down it.

It is quite possible (and highly undesirable) to get many new customers in the door and increase revenues substantially without increasing the bottom line. How? One way is to advertise that your business has the lowest prices. In general, competing with other businesses in your industry on the basis of price is a recipe for disaster. There will always be someone new coming into the arena that is able to undercut you, and you will find yourself with ever-shrinking margins and an ever-heightening battle for new customers.

Another way to lose money when your business grows is by attracting the wrong type of customers; those who need a lot of hand-holding will call you a million times for free support and advice and will waste your time in a myriad of other ways. This is time that you could have been spending giving great service to your good customers or attracting new ones.

So, when we talk about growing your business, we only want to look at *profitable* growth; growth that contributes not only to revenues, but also to the bottom line.

The Three Ways to Grow Your Business

Take a few minutes and write down all the strategies you can think of for growing your business, from advertising to networking to word-of-mouth. Anything you can think of.

_____

_____

_____

_____

_____

_____

_____

_____

_____

_____

_____

Now review your list.

Each of these strategies will fit into one of the three ways to grow your business that we will discuss in the remainder of this chapter.

The three ways to grow your business are by:

- Attracting new customers
- Selling them more
- Selling to them more often

That's it! It's not rocket science or any well-guarded management secret. All growth comes from doing one or a combination of those three things.

Let's look at each one in more detail.

Attracting new customers

If you take your list of strategies and group them by the above three ways of growing your business, you will most likely find that most of your strategies fall under the category of attracting new customers. Most small businesses focus on getting new people in the door. All the advertising you do supports this strategy; you are marketing to attract new people to try your product or service and, hopefully, to like it enough to come back again.

There are a number of reasons why focusing only on this strategy is dangerous:

- **It's expensive to market to new customers.** Your advertising budget is going to newspaper ads, telephone directory displays, and radio or television spots. It will probably cost you between 3 percent and 5 percent of your total expense budget to advertise to get new people in.

- **New customers are not yet loyal to you.** They really know nothing about you at this point. Think about a new store or service business that you have gone into lately. When you enter, you "feel out" how they do things and how they will treat you as a customer. You're willing to give them the opportunity to delight you but you are not yet willing to buy their product or service to the exclusion of all others. That's how new customers feel about you. They are taking a leap of faith to buy from you. You could spend all that money attracting them, but then some off-the-cuff remark from one of your staff could drive them back out the door.

- **It's difficult to bring new products and services to a cold market.** It takes time to build relationships with customers. Those who have known you and your business practices for a long time will be more receptive to you providing untraditional wares, but those who are new to you might be more wary and less likely to purchase anything they consider "strange."

Although it's important for every business to be able to attract new customers, smart businesses simultaneously focus on the customers they already have. These are the customers who have purchased from you before, know what you have to offer, and like it. They know you, your business practices, and your premises. Buying from you is comfortable and familiar to them. Why not ensure that you are getting the most from these customers? The last two methods of growing your business focus on these existing customers.

Selling them more

Another way to grow your business is to sell more to your existing customer base. This is also known as "up selling" and is an important part of the growth plans of companies such as McDonald's ("Would you like fries with that?") and amazon.com ("If you liked that, you'll love this").

Your current customer base knows you and likes what you have to offer. Chances are, they will like more of what you have to offer if you provide them with opportunities to buy more.

The benefits of working on this aspect of growth are:

- **Your existing customers are "warm."** They are already comfortable with the way you do business.

- **Offering more products or services to your customers will be perceived as "full service."** Customers like making multiple purchases at fewer places. It saves them time and energy in seeking out new businesses to meet their needs.

- **It's much less expensive to sell to current customers.** It can be done with the way you speak to them or with in-store displays rather than through expensive advertisements.

Selling to them more often

This strategy focuses on getting your customers to come back and buy more frequently. This may entail reminding customers of the range of products or services you provide. For example, if you are furnace repair company, remind your customers that you not only repair broken furnaces, but also provide a fall maintenance package to ensure that their furnaces are in good running condition for the upcoming winter. Give them more reasons to come back and see you.

Leverage Revisited

In the second book of the *Numbers 101 for Small Business* series, *Financial Management 101*, we touched on the concept of leverage. Here we will discuss it in detail.

The leverage that we are talking about here is not the leverage that you associate with borrowing money. This is the leverage that you achieve by focusing on all three growth strategies at the same time: attracting new customers, selling them more every time they come in your door, and selling to them more often. Instead of scrambling to meet unreasonable growth expectations in the number of new customers you are planning for, you are better off making small incremental changes in each of the three growth areas, which is usually more realistic as well. Once you have an understanding of the numbers behind the strategy, you have the power to create immense change in your business.

Let's have a look at an example to see how this works.

CASE STUDY

"Wow," Becky said. "I already have some ideas about how we can put together some service packages for our residential customers. I can't believe we've never thought of marketing to our existing customers before."

Joe said, "It's because we've always focused on advertising before. All our competitors did it so we did it too."

"Not any more," Becky said. "At least, that's not all we'll be doing. We don't want to be financially struggling like most of our competitors, and this is how we're going to grow."

Vivian said," Now let's take some time and work on new sales procedures that will help us move toward our targets."

Jason Forwell owns a small office-supplies shop. His revenues have been growing steadily over the past five years, but he is on the verge of expanding the premises into the vacant space next to his shop and he wants to grow his revenues quickly to be able to cover the costs of the move. Currently, he has approximately 275 regular customers. With the help of his accountant, he has determined that those customers come into the shop on average twice per year and they spend $125 every time they come in.

Therefore, Jason's revenues are —

275 customers X $125 every visit X 2 visits = $68,750

Jason's initial plan was to advertise heavily in the local newspaper and run radio ads on the talk radio station to bring in more customers. His goal was to increase his customer base by 25 percent. This would give him revenues of —

344 customers X $125 every visit X 2 visits = $86,000

This would represent an increase in revenue exactly equal to the increase in the customer base, or 25 percent. Jason felt that this would be enough to justify the expansion, although he was unsure as to whether it was actually possible to increase revenues by such a large percentage by advertising alone.

Jason spoke with his accountant about the plan and the accountant showed Jason that by making small changes in all three growth areas, he could have a much greater impact on revenues. Together, they mapped out the following plan:

1. Increase the customer base by 10 percent from 275 to 303. This would be accomplished through a mail-out to current customers, offering them a 10 percent discount on their next order if they bring in a new customer.

2. Increase the amount the customers spend every time they come in by 10 percent from $125 to $138. This will be accomplished through a combination of visual displays and staff script. Commonly used items such as pens, labels, and envelopes will be prominently displayed beside the cash register. Jason will prepare a training document for the shop staff pairing common items together. For example, customers purchasing printer toner cartridges may also need copy paper; customers purchasing customized letterhead may also need business cards.

3. Jason will increase the average number of times his customers come into his shop from two to three. He will do

this by surveying his customers to find out what types of goods they currently have to go to other stores to buy. For example, if Jason's shop doesn't sell office equipment, like photocopiers and printers, customers may go to a larger office supply store for those types of items. While they are there, they might also pick up some paper, computer disks, and highlighters — things that Jason does sell. Jason will find out from the surveys what he needs to stock to ensure that he keeps his customers coming back to him.

If Jason is successful in making these small incremental changes in all three of the growth strategies, this will be the impact on revenues:

303 customers X $138 per visit X 3 visits = $125,442

This represents an 82 percent increase in revenues versus the 25 percent envisioned under Jason's original strategy. It's also important to note that this type of comprehensive strategy is generally less costly and more effective to implement than advertising alone.

Now that we have had a look at the three ways to grow your business and the impact of leveraging those three ways, in the next chapter we will examine in detail how to set up your business machine to grow profitably.

Chapter Summary

➡ Before you put any growth plan in place for your business, it's important to review both your personal and business goals to ensure that the plans will integrate with each other.

➡ Growth for growth's sake is not a great business creed. It's important to seek out only profitable growth.

➡ Although there are many strategies to grow your business, they can all be grouped into only three overall methods: attracting new customers, selling them more every time they come through the door, and getting them to come through the door more often.

➡ Concentrating on all three methods simultaneously and making small incremental changes in all three will provide you with great leverage to increase your revenues.

Checklist 5
GROWING YOUR BUSINESS

1. I have prepared a business plan for my company. ❑

2. I have reviewed my profit goals to ensure they are compatible with other companies in my industry. ❑

3. I have assessed my personal need for a balance between work and family life. ❑

4. I have assessed my own risk tolerance in growing and managing my business. ❑

5. I have prepared a 12-month and 5-year revenue projection. ❑

6. I have outlined several growth strategies and have categorized them between attracting new customers, selling them more, and selling to them more often. ❑

7. I have prepared a growth plan for my business that leverages all three growth methods. ❑

Chapter

6

Getting a Handle on Your Revenues

Before we can start positioning your business for profitable growth, it's important to get a handle on where your business is at right now. In Chapter 4, we looked at your current processes and procedures to get a preliminary look at the "inner workings" of your business.

In this chapter, we want to look at your revenue streams. You may not have thought about what your historical revenues can predict for the future. By the end of this chapter, however, you will have a much deeper understanding of the money-generating side of your business.

Do you know how many customers you have in any given year? Or what they spend on average when they come to see you? Or even how often they come?

Understanding the breakdown of your current revenue stream is critical to preparing a growth plan. How will you know what needs changing if you don't know what it looks like today?

We will start by gathering as much information as possible from your historical financial information.

CASE STUDY

How Many Customers Do You Have?

If you have a business where you invoice customers in your accounting system, then you should be able to print off a listing of your current customers. If you use a manual invoicing system, however, it may take some work to come up with a customer count. Start by assembling all your invoices for the last 12 months. It doesn't matter if this time period is not the same as your fiscal year end. We are looking for the most current customer information. Sort your invoices by customer name as opposed to date. Then simply count how many different customers there are.

What do you do if you have a retail store where all your customers pay cash and you do not track their names? In this case, it pays to do a little research. For the next month, survey all customers that come into the store. Hand out a short survey form for them to fill out as your cashier is ringing up the purchases. A survey form might look like the one in Sample 1.

Keep in mind that the length of the survey can't be onerous to the customer or he or she won't participate. For example, customers in restaurants have more time to fill out a survey than convenience store customers do. Keep it short and as simple as possible.

Think about all the information this form gives you. If your customers have given you their names and addresses, you can begin a mailing list to let them know about specials and new products. Knowing if it's their first time visiting your store that month lets you know how many customers came into the store the entire month (you will simply count all the survey forms that have "yes" on this line). Knowing how many times they come in per month allows you to extrapolate how many times your customers see you every year. The final three questions give you some feedback about who your competitors actually are and how you stack up in comparison.

Once you have tracked the surveys for a month, you are ready to do your customer count. Simply count all the surveys where the customer has answered "yes" to the question "Is this your first time in the store this month?" and multiply that number by 12. For example, if 86 people said that it was their first time that month in the store, you would multiply 86 by 12 months to come up with an estimated average of 1,032 customers per year.

Sample 1
CUSTOMER SURVEY FORM

1. Name (optional): _____

2. Address (optional): _____

   _____

3. Is this your first time in the store this month? _____

4. How many times on average do you come here every month? _____

5. What other similar stores do you visit? _____

   _____

6. Is there anything that you feel we should be doing better? _____

   _____

   _____

7. What are the things that you enjoy about coming here? _____

   _____

   _____

How Often Do Your Customers Come to See You?

Now that we know how many customers we have, we need to find out how often they come to see us. If you have a computerized accounting system, such as *QuickBooks* or MYOB, this information is easily attainable. From the Reports menu, find a report that details billings by customer. Your report might look something like Sample 2. (The report was generated in *QuickBooks* so yours might look a little different.)

What we want to do with this report is to count how many invoices we have issued. Another way of getting at this information is to subtract the invoice number on your first invoice in the 12-month period from the invoice number on the last invoice in the 12-month period. For example, if your first invoice number in the year is 953 and your last one is 1712, you have issued 759 invoices

Sample 2
BILLINGS BY CUSTOMER REPORT

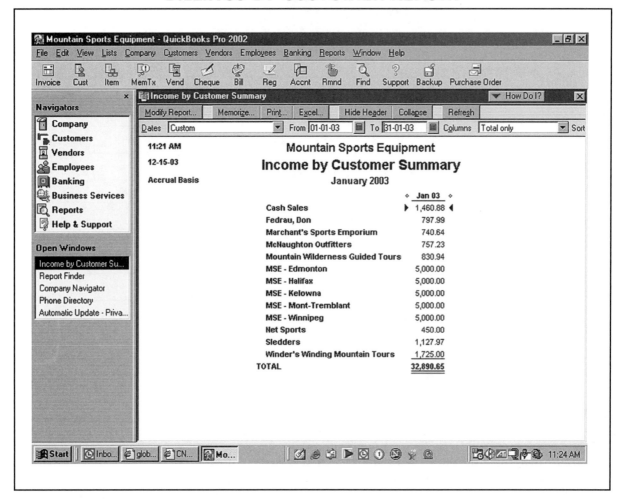

for the year. In other words, your customers have transacted with you 759 times. This second method will only work if you have issued sequential invoice numbers throughout the period and have not voided or deleted any invoices.

Once you know how many invoices you have issued in the past 12 months, simply divide that number by your customer count. Following the above example, if you have 547 customers and 759 invoices, then your customers come to see you approximately 1.4 times per year.

If you run a retail outlet, then we will go back to the survey result to come up with our estimate. You have already added up all the customers who have indicated that it is their first time that month in the store. Using only those surveys, add the cumulative number of times that these customers say they come into the store every month. Let's look at a simplified example:

Customer	1st time?	# times
John	yes	3
Mary	yes	2
Jake	yes	1
Fred	yes	6

Assuming that these are the only four customers to visit your store that month, the total number of visits is 3 + 2 + 1 + 6 = 12, and therefore, your customers visited you an average of 12/4 = 3 times that month. To get to an annual average you would multiply by 12 months. In this example, your customers would visit you an average of 3 X 12 = 36 times per year. This would be typical for a convenience or grocery store.

What Do Your Customers Spend?

Now that we know how many customers we have and how often they come to see us, we need to find out what they're spending. This is a fairly easy process for most small businesses. Review your revenues for the past 12 months. Are there any billings in there that are unusual and might spike the results? For example, did you put a special order in for a customer for a large amount of product? If this is not likely to repeat, then we want to remove it from our calculations, otherwise our averages will be unnaturally high. This process is called normalizing the revenues, or, making them normal.

Once you have what you think is a good approximation of your current revenues, divide the revenue by your customer count. For example, if you have 650 customers and your revenues last year were $127,500, then your average revenue per customer is —

$127,500/650 = $196.15 annual revenue per customer

One more calculation needs to be added, however, to get to the revenue per transaction as opposed to the revenue per customer. You now divide your revenue per customer by the average number of times your customers come to see you. Following the above

example, if your customers come to see you an average of 3.2 times per year, your average transaction is:

$$\$196.15/3.2 = \$61.30 \text{ per transaction}$$

Therefore, in this example, you have 650 customers who come to see you an average of 3.2 times per year and they spend an average of $61.30 every time they come to see you.

What Kind of Customers Do You Have?

All small businesses go through it at some point or another. They have to face a customer that they just can't make happy regardless of how much they try. Some customers are just destined to complain, berate, not pay in a timely manner, and waste your time. Unfortunately, if you are like many small businesses, you will spend proportionately more time with this type of customer trying to pacify and satisfy him or her. The customer is always right, right?

Not necessarily. Take a few moments and jot down some notes about your ideal customer. What would make him or her ideal? Here are some things that my clients tell me are important to them:

- Paying on time without being reminded
- Being appreciative of the work you've done on their behalf
- Not complaining continually
- Recommending you to others
- Not being price-sensitive (understanding value)
- Making the work you do for them as easy as possible for you

Pull out your customer list again and review it. Place an "A" beside all of your customers that most closely resemble your ideal customer. Now place a "D" beside those customers that make you cringe when they walk through the door or call you on the phone. These customers are the opposite of your "A" customers. Of those customers that are left on your list, break them into two categories, "B" and "C", depending on whether they are closer to your "A" customers or your "D" customers respectively.

Obviously, you want to concentrate on your "A" and "B" customers. These are the customers that pay well, don't complain, and, best of all, refer other "A" and "B" customers to you. Spending your time with the "D" customers, however, hinders your ability to do this.

What would your business be like if your "D" customers went to one of your competitors? I know, that's not a very nice thing to do to another business! The thought of these customers leaving may scare you at first; nobody likes to lose a customer, but think about how much more free time you would have to be able to service your "A" and "B" customers. You'll also have more time to plan and strategize to make sure that your growth plan is working. Not to mention the fact that you will see morale in your business increase once the "problem" customers are out the door. I have seen this happen dozens of times over.

Fire Away!

So, what do you do about your "D" customers? Fire them! You heard me right: fire them. You *do* have the ability to not agree to provide products or services to anyone you choose. Sample 3 is an example of a letter you can adapt to your own needs to send to those customers with whom you do not wish to do business any longer.

Once you have weeded out your more difficult customers, you will be well positioned to start growing your business with many more "A" and "B" customers. The improvement to the bottom line will be staggering!

The Next Step

In this chapter, we have learned how to get a handle on our historical customer information. Now is a good time to assess whether your accounting software is giving you the type of information that you need to run your business effectively. You will need to access this type of financial information on a regular basis. If you need to upgrade your record keeping software, you may wish to refer back to the first book in the *Numbers 101 for Small Business* series, *Bookkeepers' Boot Camp* for a fuller discussion of some considerations that you need to take into account as you are selecting a new system.

Now that we understand where our business has been in the past and we have weeded out the "bad apples," it's time to start our growth plan and test the impact that those changes have made.

Chapter Summary

➡ Your revenue stream is made up of a combination of how many customers you have, how often they come to see you, and how much they spend every time they come through the door.

➡ For most small businesses (except retail), your bookkeeping system should provide all the information you need to analyze your revenue streams.

➡ Consider weeding out your "D" quality customers to free up more of your time for planning and strategizing.

➡ Consider upgrading your bookkeeping system if information about revenues is not readily accessible.

Sample 3
TERMINATING A CUSTOMER

15 January 20—

Mr. John Doe
275 Clutterbuck Place
Joshua, MN 99506

Dear John,

There are times when every business needs to take some time and review their interactions with their customers, as well as look towards the future path.

That is what we have done here at McManus Computer Consultants. We have reviewed the products and services that we have traditionally provided to our customers and we have made some difficult decisions.

We have come to the realization that in order to provide the best and most comprehensive service to our customers, we must offer more services to fewer customers.

We have reviewed the history of the services that we have provided to you since you have been with us and we feel that your needs would be best served by another computer consulting firm. We would be happy to refer you to one if you wish.

We wish you all the best in the future!

Sincerely,

Michael McManus

McManus Computer Consultants

Checklist 6
GETTING A HANDLE ON YOUR REVENUES

1. I have set up a system to track information about my customers: their frequency, their purchases, and their habits. ❑

2. I know how many customers I have. ❑

3. I know how much my customers spend on average. ❑

4. I know how often my customers come to my business. ❑

5. I have rated my customers based on criteria such as the ease of serving them, the amount they spend, and their payment and referral history. ❑

6. I have considered firing my less desirable customers. ❑

7. I have reviewed my initial choice of accounting software and have ensured that it still meets my needs. ❑

Chapter

7

Your Strategy

We have spent a great deal of time so far in this book laying the foundation for growth. This is time well spent because many small businesses make the mistake of growing unchecked without any idea as to where they've been or where they are going. We started by looking at the benefits of "systematizing" our business: developing processes and procedures that can be followed and duplicated with consistency. We then reviewed our business and personal goals to make sure that our growth plan will dovetail with those goals. We've looked at the importance of profitable growth as well as the quality of our customers. Now we are finally ready to put our growth plan in place, from the top down.

Your Business's Vision Statement

Your business's vision statement formalizes those business goals that we discussed in Chapter 5. The vision statement is an overall picture of what the business will look like in the future. It addresses who you are, what you're about, and how you will get there. Sample 4 gives two examples of effective vision statements.

First, the vision statement talks about the niche that the business will occupy. Are you the most knowledgeable? Or the most full-service? Do you have the widest selection? This is your niche and will be an integral part of your vision.

Sample 4
VISION STATEMENTS

Vision Statement 1

In ten years, we will be the most recognized computer consulting firm in our area of operation. Our revenues will grow to $1.2 million and we will maintain an aggressive growth rate of 20 percent per year, focusing only on profitable growth. The firm will be a fun place to work for both owners and employees. Employees will be compensated based on performance and alignment to the vision statement. The firm will hire only the best and brightest in the computer consulting field and these employees will receive outstanding training and work experience as well as long-term growth opportunities. All of this will be accomplished with absolute integrity and fairness to all those who interact with us.

Vision Statement 2

Kelly's Convenience store will be Kensington Market's neighborhood grocery. We will stock a wide variety of products needed by customers on a regular basis and we will carry only the freshest fruits and vegetables. Our employees will be friendly and knowledgeable and will actively assist customers with their grocery purchases. Our loyal customer base will grow by 15 percent per year as new customers move into the area and as the neighborhood grows to value the store.

Second, the vision statement outlines in general terms how the business will accomplish its goals. What is it that will make you the best? How will you meet your customers' expectations? The vision statement is the skin in which your business will operate in the future. Its audience is the business owner, the employees, the customers, and the suppliers, in short, everyone who comes into contact with the business.

The Mission Statement

The purpose of the mission statement is to bring the general values of the vision statement down into measurable, concrete goals. In order for a mission statement to be effective, it needs to meet six criteria. Your mission statement must be —

- **Measurable.** You need to be able to determine if the goals are being met on a regular basis.

- **Challenging.** The goals should be a stretch to reach, but not unrealistic or unattainable.

- **Focused.** You will be using the mission statement to make operational and strategic decisions in your business so the goals need to be sharply focused.

- **Flexible.** The goals should allow for individual interpretation within the framework originally envisioned.

- **Clear.** One of the most important facets of the mission statement is its ability to be explained and understood by everyone in the organization. Therefore the goals should be easy to understand and not marred with "business speak."

- **Appropriate.** The goals in the mission statement must work towards achievement of the vision statement. If the mission statement is not in perfect alignment with the vision statement, the overall goals will not be achieved and the business will be dysfunctional.

Sample 5 shows a mission statement related to the vision of the computer consulting firm above.

Notice how the mission statement in Sample 5 takes each item in the vision statement and tells "how" the business is going to meet its vision goals. Once your mission statement has been developed, it needs to be drilled down even farther into individual operational tasks.

CASE STUDY

Becky made a face. "A vision statement? That sounds so formal! Do we really have to go through all that for such a small business?"

"The whole point is that you will be growing into a much larger business," said Vivian, "and it's important to lay the groundwork properly. We've already analyzed where you've been, now we have to look forward to where you're going."

Joe said, "Well, we already know that we want to have a million dollars in revenue in ten years and that we will be growing 18 percent per year to do that. That's a start."

"Yes," said Vivian, "now let's talk about your business's community profile and services. Let's look at what Joe's Plumbing stands for."

Sample 5
MISSION STATEMENT

1. In ten years, we will be the most recognized computer consulting firm in our area of operation.

   We will develop and maintain a highly visible community presence and will be known as a community-based business.

   Our marketing and promotional material will be distinctive and will be highly visible in all of our customers' places of business.

2. Our revenues will grow to $1.2 million and we will maintain an aggressive growth rate of 20 percent per year, focusing only on profitable growth.

   We will actively seek new customers through our interactions with our existing customers.

   We will strive to provide the best service to our select group of customers, turning them into not only loyal customers, but also advocates for us.

3. Our firm will be a fun place to work for both owners and employees.

   We will solicit employee feedback and input on all business matters.

   We will create a casual yet professional working environment where employees feel comfortable and productive.

4. Employees will be compensated based on performance and alignment with the vision statement.

   We will develop and maintain a world-class performance and evaluation system in which employees participate in both the risks and rewards of the business.

   We will clearly communicate our vision and mission statements with all employees on a regular basis.

5. The firm will hire only the best and brightest in the computer consulting field, and these employees will receive outstanding training and work experience as well as long-term growth opportunities.

   We will become the computer consulting firm of choice for new college graduates and those seeking employment in our industry.

Sample 5 — Continued

> We will develop and maintain a world-class employee training system as well as thorough and clear documentation of every process and procedure in the business.
>
> 6. All of this will be accomplished with absolute integrity and fairness to all those who interact with the business.
>
> We will review our operations on a monthly basis with all employees.
>
> We will send feedback request forms to all customers at least annually to ensure that the customers' needs are being not only met, but also surpassed.

Your Operational Plan

In order for the mission statement goals to be implemented consistently, it's important to break them down even further into individual tasks with the names of the employees whose responsibility is to carry out each one, as well as specific timelines and measurements.

Let's have a look at the first mission statement goal in Sample 5. The associated operational tasks might look like this:

1. We will develop and maintain a highly visible community presence and will be known as a community-based business.

2. We will enter a corporate team in the Chamber of Commerce charity relay annually.

3. We will develop and maintain a charitable giving program whereby all donations made through the program by our customers or employees are matched by the business. This program will be put in place by April 30.

4. We will actively seek other opportunities to provide a visible community presence and will solicit input from our employees.

Notice how the mission statement goal has been broken down further to tell exactly how the business will accomplish the goal. These operational goals should become a part of the management operational plan that is followed on a consistent basis. See the second book in the *Numbers 101 for Small Business* series, *Financial Management 101,* for a fuller discussion of developing the management operational plan.

CASE STUDY

Becky finished reading the final draft of the vision statement out loud to Joe and Vivian.

"I feel like we're a bigger business already," Joe said. "But it's going to take a lot of work to become the business that's on that piece of paper."

Vivian said, "You're right, Joe. It will take a lot of work. But you have the framework in place already. Now we have to break the vision down into its component parts."

Vision Statement

Joe's Plumbing will provide its customers with top-notch service, as evidenced by its highly skilled plumbers helping customers in a polite and efficient manner. We will be the largest locally owned plumbing business in the tri-state area with annual revenues of over $1 million.

All Joe's Plumbing team members will work in an environment filled with mutual respect, trust, and absolute fun. All team members will be compensated well, based on individual and team performance, and will have access to continuous training and learning.

Chapter Summary

➡ Before your growth plan is put in place, it's important to make sure that the plan will help you meet your business and personal goals.

➡ Your vision statement is an umbrella statement that represents your business goals.

➡ Your mission statement takes the overall vision and breaks it into concrete, measurable pieces.

➡ The mission statement is further broken down into operational tasks, with deadlines and responsibilities attached.

Checklist 7
YOUR STRATEGY

1. I have articulated the niche in which my business operates. ❏

2. I have analyzed my company's unique qualities in relation to my competitors. ❏

3. I have developed and recorded a formal vision statement for my business. ❏

4. I have broken the general values in my vision statement down into measurable, concrete goals in my mission statement. ❏

5. I have reviewed my monthly management operating plan to ensure that it fits in with the company's mission and vision statements. ❏

6. I have assigned responsibilities and deadlines to all tasks in my management operating plan. ❏

7. I have set up a review system to ensure that the tasks assigned in my management operating plan get completed. ❏

Testing Change

In the last chapter, we stressed the importance of having measurable goals so that you know if you are in alignment with the business's vision. In this chapter, we look at how to test and measure your growth plan and what to do if it needs adjustment.

Not understanding what impact every facet of their business has on profitability contributes to the downfall of thousands of businesses every year. Most small-business owners rely on their own faulty intuition or "gut feel" about what effect a new ad or a new product will have on their customers or revenues. Marketers often say, "I know I'm wasting half of my advertising dollars. I just don't know which half." This attitude results in overspending on marketing and promotion in an effort to hit the target with a "splatter gun" approach.

Measuring the results of changes in your business is the only way to know that you are still on the right path. It allows you to zero in on the least expensive and most productive growth strategies. You can measure everything, including prices, advertising, sales presentation methods, employee compensation packages, and the mix of products and services that you offer. A business should integrate continual measuring and testing its entire life. That will ensure that the business continually grows and improves over time. Let's look at some of the different areas where measuring and testing are critical.

Advertising

Print and radio advertising can be the most expensive part of your marketing and promotion campaign. And if you're large enough to have a television advertising budget, well, the cost can be astronomical.

It doesn't seem to make sense, then, that most small businesses never know what, if any, benefits they are getting from their advertising campaigns. The cost of this ignorance can be enormous. It is estimated that one-half to two-thirds of all advertising dollars may just as well have been set on fire with a match!

Let's start with the basics: Do you know where your new customers are coming from? Telephone book ads? Word of mouth? Networking? For example, let's say you were spending $2,000 per year to have a display ad in the telephone book. Through analyzing your customer base and finding out where customers first heard about your business, you discover that only three percent of your customers found you in the telephone book. Most of your customers come in through referrals from existing customers or other associates. What impact will this have on your advertising budget? Are you likely to spend $2,000 next year to get only a few more customers? Not likely. You will have saved that $2,000 from going up in smoke and will still have almost the same number of customers. This illustrates why testing and measuring the results of your advertising campaigns can be very lucrative for your business.

Once you know where your customers are coming from, it's time to analyze the effectiveness of how you market to them. If most of your customers come in through referrals, one of your growth strategies may be to actively pursue your business contacts to solicit referrals. It's important to know how effective this change has been on your number of customers and your revenue. For example, let's say you send a mailing to your existing customers with a business card and an offer of 50 percent off their next visit to you if they bring in a new customer. It's a very simple matter of tracking how many new customers come in as referrals of existing customers. If your program only results in one new customer for every 100 letters you send to existing customers, then you know that the campaign has not been very effective. This will let you modify the campaign to improve its effectiveness. Try it again with 75 percent off the next visit or change the wording of the letter. But remember to only change one variable at a time so that you know when you've hit upon a winning idea.

This also works with print, radio, and television advertising. Every piece of advertising should be measurable. It is a well-known marketing truism that different headlines can have a dramatic impact on customer responses. Test the effectiveness of your headlines, make changes, and test again. See how many responses the ads pull and what the conversion ratio is. (The conversion ratio is the number of inquiries from the ad that turn into paying customers. We will cover this concept in more detail in Chapter 10.).

If you are running different ad campaigns, have a unique identifier so that you know from which initiative the customer arrives. For example, you can include a coupon that must be returned. The coupons in each campaign would be unique, so that you can see that, for example, 20 new customers came from this ad and 57 came from that ad. You could also set up a different toll-free number for the potential customers to call depending on which ad they are responding to.

If you think that these measurement and testing techniques are too time-consuming or expensive, think about how much business and advertising money you are losing because you don't know what works.

Prices

When it comes to testing prices, many small-business owners put on the brakes. "Oh no, we have to charge this. If we change our prices, we'll lose all our business to our competitors." Again, this is a "gut feel" statement and may not bear any relation to facts.

The price that you charge for your product or service relates to the value equation: Value = Benefits/Cost. (We will discuss this value equation in more detail in Chapter 9.)

The more perceived benefits to the customer versus the cost of the product or service, the higher the value the customer will place on it. Many small businesses tend to undervalue their own products and services and charge too little for the value the customer receives.

There is another variable in the value perception, however. It is the perception that cheaper goods are low quality. Let me give you the real-life example of one of my clients.

Jim (not his real name) owns a small café in the trendy Queen Street West area of Toronto. He has 11 tables and a bar area. When Jim took over the business from the retiring owner, at first he kept everything the same. The menu had changed little in almost 20 years.

The café served diner-style food: large servings, simple ingredients, low prices. The area that Jim had turned into a bar had been a lunch counter. The restaurant was frequently operating at capacity. The tables were always full at both lunch and dinner. By most accounts, the restaurant was a huge success. The problem that jumped out at Jim after a short while was that his profits were dismal. He was paying an exorbitant rent typical for that neighborhood. He just wasn't able to turn over the tables fast enough to meet his costs. Something had to change quickly.

Jim was acutely aware of the value equation. He knew that the area in Toronto that he was operating in was famous as a "destination." People browse Queen West for its trendy bars, art galleries, and clubs. The popularity of the area and its reputation was one of the reasons that Jim's rent was so high.

Ultimately, Jim knew that he had to change his prices to be able to survive. He knew that this meant that people's perceptions of the cafe had to change. The first thing he did was to paint and renovate the interior to reflect a comfortable but upscale environment. He applied for and received a liquor license and converted the lunch counter into a bar and lounge area. The next thing he did was to consult with his kitchen staff about the menu. Jim knew that he wanted to offer customers a better dining experience and thereby be able to command higher prices.

In the end, Jim altered the menu to include many dishes that still had simple ingredients but were prepared in a more "upscale" fashion and had "trendier" names. He was able to increase his prices by an average of 112 percent with only an additional 16 percent in cost. And the cafe was still full every lunch and dinner. Had Jim not been successful in his first testing of his price changes, he would have adjusted the menu and pricing again until it had the desired effect on revenues. Jim has since purchased four other restaurants in Toronto and has revamped them in a similar manner. In three of these cases, he had to alter his original plan based on testing his prices. With all five of his restaurants, he will continually test his strategies and make the changes he needs to always be improving quality and the bottom line.

It's important to remember that, for example, a 10 percent increase in prices does not always equate to an equal and offsetting decrease in customers. You need to test the changes that you can make in prices without losing business.

Environment

The environment in which you and your employees work can have a huge impact on your revenues, both from an internal and an external perspective. Internally, how your employees feel about coming to work every day can affect their morale and motivation — which can affect how they do their jobs and interrelate with customers. Externally, customers make unconscious conclusions about a business by the environment in which it operates.

The example that I will give you about internal environment issues relates to my own experience. While I was articling with accounting firms to receive my accounting designation, I worked in some very different environments. Some of the firms were extremely informal: They were loud and raucous, had no dress code, and had a refrigerator full of beer. There was no hierarchy and employees had complete freedom to manage our own time. Some of the firms were diametrically opposite: They were silent, formal environments where employees did not speak to the partners unless it was vital. We wore formal business attire and spoke with fellow workers with short monotone sentences, always related to work, never to hockey or reality TV shows or our families.

Both of the extremes in which I worked affected the firms. In a completely anarchistic workplace, it is sometimes difficult to switch from being laid back and informal to listening to client needs and being respectful. On the other hand, in a rigid, severe atmosphere, a client may perceive us as being rigid in our thinking and advice. When I started my own accounting firm, I tried to strike a balance between these models: informal enough to encourage original thought, but structured enough to focus on client needs. I tested and adjusted the rules for our working environment until the business was successful, as evidenced by employee retention and client happiness.

The external environment can have an even more direct impact on the operations and, ultimately, revenues of a business. Customers make subconscious conclusions about the quality and professionalism of a business by the first impressions formed when first entering the business's environment.

The next time you walk into a new business, whether it be a retail store, a supplier or your local dry cleaners, consciously think about the first impressions that form as you enter. Is the entry area clean and tidy? What do you smell? Is the area set up for the benefit of the customer or the staff? Is the waiting area soothing, with

CASE STUDY

"I never knew that the telephone company can set up a separate telephone number for new customers to call us," said Becky.

"Yes," said Vivian. "They will also provide you with a report to let you know how many customers used that telephone number, which also tells you how many customers called because of that ad."

"That's great," Becky said. "Then we know if it's worth all that money. We can finally figure out if our advertising dollars are paying off."

Joe sat down heavily. "I don't know if I'm ready to give customers surveys and find out what they think about Joe's Plumbing."

"It will be really enlightening, Joe," Becky said. "We want to know what they think before they go and tell all their friends. If we're doing something right, it shows us so that we can keep doing it. If we're doing something wrong, we can fix it."

➡ You can't know if your business is on the right track unless you test and measure every change you make to your operations.

➡ You can measure the effectiveness of your advertising by having unique response coupons or codes so that you can tell from which piece of advertising a response comes.

➡ The impact of changes to prices can be measured directly by their impact on revenues.

➡ The way your customers perceive your environment can also be measured by informally tracking customer comments or formally tracking survey responses.

soft colors and calming music, or chaotic, with ringing telephones and employees yelling? Businesses that make the effort to set up their operations for the benefit and comfort of their customers develop loyal customers.

How can you do this in your own business? First, think about how you like to be welcomed into the companies with which you interact. What does the environment look like? What sounds and smells greet you? Incorporate these elements into your own business and test the response. There are many ways to do this, but these are the two main ones:

- Track comments made by customers when they enter the environment for the first time. If it's a positive environment, you may hear comments such as "Take your time. I'm enjoying the wait." or "I always feel so comfortable here." Although these are subjective measures of success, they are still important to track.

- Solicit more formal feedback. At the end of every customer interaction, provide a short survey for customers to fill out, indicating anything they particularly enjoyed or wanted to have changed concerning many aspects of your business, including the operating environment.

If you find that customers do not talk about the comfort of your environment, through either informal conversation or formal survey, make changes to the environment and test again. Continue to improve and retest until your test results cannot be improved by any other changes you make. This way, you'll always be improving your customers' impressions of your business and will be making changes when necessary.

Checklist 8
TESTING CHANGE

1. I know from where my new customers are being referred. ❑

2. I know how many new customers each of my advertising and marketing campaigns are yielding. ❑

3. I have developed a system to measure the response to every new advertising initiative. ❑

4. I have reviewed all of the prices of my goods and services to ensure that they will meet market expectations. ❑

5. I have thought about the type of atmosphere in which I want my staff to operate and which I want clients to experience. ❑

6. I have documented the specific tasks related to my marketing and promotional strategy. ❑

7. I have documented the specific tasks related to making the operating environment of my business comfortable and hospitable to staff and customers. ❑

Chapter
9

Your Product or Service

In this chapter, we are going to look at your offerings as a business, regardless of whether you offer a product or service. *What* you offer and *how* you present it can make a substantial difference in your revenues. Remember from Chapter 5 that the three ways to grow a business are —

- Attract new customers
- Sell them more every time they come
- Get them to come more often

Also, remember that, in order to get leveraged growth, we need to concentrate simultaneously on all three areas.

Why Should Customers Buy from You?

This is a question that you have asked yourself as part of developing your vision and mission statements (see Chapter 7). What makes you different from your competitors and sets you apart? When potential customers consider making a new purchase, why would they consider your business? There are really only two bases upon which you can compete in business: price and value.

Competing on price

"THE LOWEST PRICE IN TOWN"

"WE MATCH ALL COMPETITORS' PRICES"

"NOBODY BEATS US . . . NOBODY!"

CASE STUDY

"Ok. So now can we start actually working on our growth plan?" Joe asked.

"Joe, don't be so impatient," Becky said. "It takes time to do things the right way. Remember, we want to grow this company into a million-dollar asset." She turned to Vivian. "But I'm really looking forward to actually putting this plan in place."

Vivian sipped her coffee. "We're just about there. We know how much we're going to grow and the basics of how to grow. Now we need to have a look at the services that you provide to your customers and see where you can increase sales."

Joe frowned. "How can we do that? The way it works is that, if customer need plumbing work done, they call us. We can't predict when someone's drain is going to back up."

Vivian said, "Let's start by making a list of all the services that you have provided over the last year. I think you'll find some interesting patterns emerging."

I'm sure you've seen headlines like this in the advertising section of your local newspaper. In fact, take a few minutes right now and look through the sales flyers in the newspaper. How many businesses are advertising that their price is the best?

Many small businesses feel that they have to compete on price alone; that customers will only come and buy from you if you are the cheapest. What this ends up doing is starting a downward cycle, where each business in an industry undercuts the other until there are no margins left, and businesses start going bankrupt or leaving the industry.

If you think that you can undercut all your competitors, think again. There will always be new competitors in the market who can undercut you. New competitors have the benefit of still having their start-up financing in place and can price almost at cost for however long they feel it will take to yank your customer base out from under you.

Something else to consider is that the type of customer that buys from you solely on price will jump to a competitor in a heartbeat if the competitor's prices are lower. There is no customer loyalty at this end of the market. It can make for some very hard slogging on your part just to keep your proverbial head above water if you are going to compete on price.

Competing on value

The other niche upon which you can base your business is adding value. We discussed this concept briefly in Chapter 8. By far, the largest segment of consumers doesn't simply want the cheapest price regardless. They want to know that they are getting value for their money. It's not that they want to pay more if they don't have to, but they understand that cheaper isn't always better. Customers define value as:

Benefits/Price

The higher the perceived benefits to the customer versus the price of a product or service, the more likely he or she is to purchase. Notice that we are speaking of "perceived benefits." That means that the customer needs to believe he or she is getting the best product or service for the best price. Getting that value perception across to customers is one of the most important jobs of a business.

My experience has shown me that most small businesses are terrified to compete on value, because it is so ingrained in them that they have to cut prices to stay in business. But think about how wonderful it would be to get a higher price for your product or service, provide better quality to your customers, and have them appreciate what you provide to them. That's the outcome of competing on value.

How Is Your Business Different?

Consumer theory shows that customers buy value that they perceive. What this means is that if they feel that the benefits of your product or service outweigh its cost by a higher margin than your competitors (assuming, of course, that it's a product or service that they need), then they will buy that perceived value. Remember from the above section that value to a customer is defined as:

Benefits/Price

Articulating your product or service's value, however, runs much deeper than your advertising campaign. It needs to be at the heart of your business. It is embedded in your vision and mission statements, and it needs to be communicated indirectly to customers through every interaction that you have with them.

Does the value you bring to the table have to be completely different than any other business in your industry? Of course not. You simply have to articulate it better.

For example, FedEx's slogan (and, in fact, the core of their entire business) is —

Absolutely Positively Overnight

Are they the only courier company on the planet that can deliver packages overnight? Of course not! But they articulate it better than anyone else. It's clear to their customers and potential customers that they will get it there by tomorrow morning. And, of course, that's extremely important to customers of the courier industry.

So, how can you articulate the value that your business provides? What makes you stand out from your competitors? Do you have the most experience in the industry? Are you the most full-service?

Once you have determined your value statement, make sure that it permeates all your correspondence and internal processes and procedures. Make it the very core of your operations.

Let's look at some hands-on ways that you can increase your revenues by focusing on your customers' perceived value of your product or service.

Selling a Product

In general, it is easier to communicate to potential customers the value of a product than of a service. Customers can see and touch your product and will be able to compare it to the products your competitor offers.

However, it's critical to continually remind your customers and potential customers of the benefits of owning your product. For example, if you sell vacuum cleaners, remind them that, if they buy your vacuum cleaner, they —

- will never have to change a bag,
- will be able to vacuum their curtains with the special attachment, thereby saving money on dry cleaning, and
- will be able to tuck it away in a very small space when done, thereby saving them space.

It's an old marketing truism that customers buy benefits, not features, and it's a valuable one. What it means is, that instead of listing all the bells and whistles of your product, tell your customers why they should care. Lead them by the hand to show them how much better their lives would be if only they owned your product. The benefits can even be ones that the customer would get if they bought your competitors' products. But if you're the company that can articulate those benefits the best, you will get the business.

Up Selling

You most likely have come across this term before. It means offering the customer more. McDonald's uses this strategy hundreds of thousands of times every day, whenever an employee says, "Would you like fries with that?"

To see another example, look at the area surrounding the checkout counter at any grocery store. The area will be filled with common useful items that almost everyone needs: batteries, light bulbs, camera film, and candy bars (okay, this one technically isn't a need, but it's something that people grab on impulse, especially if they are stuck in a checkout line). The grocery store is giving its customers one last opportunity to buy from them.

Take some time to examine the products that you offer and then list the related products and supplies that you could be offering. If you sell cameras, your customers will also need film, photo processing, frames, lenses, and camera bags. If these customers have to go elsewhere for these supplies, you are letting money walk out the door. They are already in front of you — do not be afraid to sell more to them.

You can also package these products together. In our camera example, instead of slashing the price of the camera to bring people in the door (competing on price), offer them a special deal: If they buy a camera from you, they will get a free camera bag and two rolls of film. This is showing the customer the value that they will receive. You will end up with much more revenue than you would if you simply cut your prices.

Providing a Service

Articulating the value of a service can be more difficult than doing so for a product. A product is tangible; it is something a customer can touch, see, and smell. They can assess the value fairly quickly and easily. A service, on the other hand, is intangible. When it has been completed, it may be difficult for the customer to know what value has been added. Therefore, it's critical to make sure that you define and communicate the value of your services.

Let's look at an example of two companies in the same industry: landscaping. You are in need of some landscaping services around your house. You definitely need the grass cut on a regular basis and you might want some help with weeding flower beds and some ongoing lawn fertilizing and maintenance.

You call Lawn King, the first landscaping company listed in the Yellow Pages. This is the information they tell you over the telephone about their services:

- Lawn cutting costs $40 per hour. There is a minimum one-hour charge per cut and a minimum charge of $400 per year.
- Weeding and landscaping services cost $75 per hour. There is a minimum two-hour charge per visit.
- Other lawn maintenance services are by quotation and dependent upon the size of yard.

You then call Landscapes Galore to see how their services and prices stack up. They give you this information:

Lawn care package:
- Weekly lawn cutting from April to October
- Spring revitalization treatment including aerating, organic fertilizer, and weed removal

CASE STUDY

- Fall maintenance treatment including de-thatching and rooting fertilizer
- Cost: $375 due April 1 or four monthly payments of $100 beginning April 1
- Other services: Flower bed design consultation — $125
- Winter snow removal November to March — $225

Now, which company are you more likely to hire? The second one of course, and you may even decide to have them do your snow removal in the winter. Landscapes Galore has "productized" their service, which means that they have tried to make it as tangible as possible. They give you a fixed price and clearly state what you get for that price. Not only that, but they also clearly tell you what other bundles of services they provide to make it easier for you to decide whether or not you need those services.

The first company, Lawn King, is typical of many small businesses. They are so afraid of losing money on a sale that they hedge their bets. They quote by the hour and put in minimums. They also won't quote on other jobs without coming out to see them. The problem with this approach is that it makes the potential customer wary. The customer is not sure of the final bill and is therefore more reluctant to hire the company. What if it takes them six hours to cut the lawn!

How can you make your service more like a product? Consider the following strategy:

1. List all the services you provide or could provide. Only include those services that you and your staff are skilled at and enjoy doing.

2. Put together some "packages" of services that you feel would be of interest to your customers. Take some time to think about what your customers' needs are.

3. Work out what you feel would be the average charge to perform all these services. Look at how much time you think it would take to provide the services and price accordingly.

4. Communicate the packages to your existing customers. Let them know what else they can buy from you. They already like what you have to offer and they trust your quality and business ethics.

You can put a stronger push on these packages during your slow operating periods. For example, if your revenues are seasonal and usually decrease in the summer, offer the packages of services during that time to smooth out and boost your revenue streams.

Teaching Your Customers

Whether you sell a product or a service, one way you might consider adding to your revenues is by running workshops for your customers. People like to learn how to do things for themselves rather than being reliant upon others. This strategy can work in almost every industry. If you sell vacuums, you can run a half-day workshop on extending the life of your carpet. If you run a computer consulting business, you can teach customers more advanced computing skills, how to set up their own data base, or a myriad of other computer skills. Customers will value learning these skills and you can price your workshops accordingly. It's a great way to boost your revenue throughout the year.

Checklist 9
YOUR PRODUCT OR SERVICE

1. I am able to articulate why my customers should buy from me rather than the competition. ❑

2. I have ensured that my growth strategy is based on competing on value, not on price. ❑

3. I have reviewed all of my marketing and promotional material to make sure that they embody the value that my product or services bring to my customers. ❑

4. I have analyzed which of my products or services are a natural fit with each other. ❑

5. I have documented my plan for presenting products and services to my customers that are a natural fit with the ones they are purchasing. ❑

6. I have "productized" the services I offer so that customers can easily see their value. ❑

7. I have considered providing training courses to my customers as an added source of revenue. ❑

Your Customer Interactions

You can have the best product or service on earth and still not be able to attract or retain customers if you and your employees fail to develop good customer service skills. I'm talking about more than just being nice to people. I'm talking about the way customers view every single interaction with your business. How you interact with your customers can make a huge impact on your number of customers and the amount of revenue that they generate.

Telephone Interactions

Most small businesses are dependent upon the telephone to conduct their business and interact with customers and potential customers. Sample 6 shows two examples of how a small business might answer the telephone when a potential customer phones to inquire about the services the company offers.

Although these two telephone conversations are fictional, they are representative of the differences between businesses that do and do not understand the importance of every customer interaction.

Which business are you more likely to deal with? The second one, most likely. The employee was personable, knowledgeable, and helpful. He also knew the importance of closing the deal.

Sample 6
TELEPHONE INTERACTIONS

Situation 1

Employee: Taylor Hardware.

Caller: Yes, hi. Could you tell me if you have any 12-foot 4X4 cedar in stock?

Employee: Uh, yeah. We usually have some around.

Caller: And how much is it?

Employee: (shuffling paper) Uh, I think it's $37.50.

Caller: Thanks.

Employee hangs up.

Situation 2

Employee: Good morning, Greenplay Hardware, this is James.

Caller: Hi, James, could you tell me if you have any 12-foot 4X4 cedar in stock?

Employee: Sure, thanks for calling. It will just take me a moment to look it up on the screen. While I'm doing that, can I ask what type of project you need it for?

Caller: I'm building a swing set for my kids. I have all the other wood, just not the crossbar.

Employee: That sounds like an ambitious project! Just to let you know, we've just gotten in some new rope ladders that would be a great addition to any swing set. When you drop in, just ask for me and I'd be happy to show them to you. Ah, here it is: 12-foot 4X4 cedar. We have over a dozen in stock. They're $37.50 each. Would you like me to set one aside for you?

Caller: Sure, that would be great. The last name is Jones. I'll be in this afternoon and I would definitely like to see those rope ladders.

Employee: Great. When you come in I will show you how to attach the ladder. It's really quite simple.

Caller: Thanks, James. I'll see you this afternoon.

Employee: Have a great day, Mr. Jones.

The Art of Closing the Deal

When we look at the first of the three ways to grow your business (see Chapter 5), attracting new customers, we can break that down further into two categories:

- Getting more potential customers in front of you
- Converting more potential customers into buyers

Let's say that you run a restaurant. More than 95 percent of your business comes from people calling in to make reservations. People who have never been in your restaurant before, however, want to ask some questions over the telephone before they decide that they want to make a reservation. They generally inquire about prices, seating, noise level, and menu.

Currently, out of every ten potential new customers who call, six make a reservation. This is your conversion ratio. The conversion ratio is calculated as:

Conversion ratio = People who buy/People who inquire

Your conversion rate is therefore six divided by ten, or 60 percent. Your goal is to get more new customers who will come back again and again. There are two ways that you can get more new customers to make reservations:

1. You can get more people to call the restaurant.
2. You can convert more of the telephone inquiries into reservations.

Let's look at each of these in turn.

Getting more people to call

You can get more people to call your business through advertising or giving out coupons. One restaurant client of mine turns her existing customers into sales people for the restaurant. Current customers receive a free meal if they convince a friend or associate who has never been in the restaurant before to make a reservation. At first, you might think: Well, that doesn't do me any good. I'm losing the revenue on one meal to get the revenue on another. But, if you look at the long-term potential of a new customer, you will realize that you are gaining a whole lot more. We will talk about the lifetime customer in Chapter 11.

Going back to our example, let's say in an average month, you have 75 potential new customers call the restaurant to make

CASE STUDY

"Hello. Joe's Plumbing," Becky said in answer to the ring of the telephone.

"Yes. My husband and I are building an addition on to our house. We're doing the general contracting ourselves and we need a plumber to come in to put in the fixtures in the new bathroom. Do you do that type of work?"

"Absolutely." Becky began to take notes.

"How much do you charge?"

"We charge $40 per hour. If you need a better idea of the cost, I can send Joe out to look at it for you."

"Um … does that visit cost anything?"

Becky answered, "No. Not at all."

"Well, let me discuss it with my husband and I'll get back to you."

"Okay. Thanks. Bye."

Becky hung up the phone. It would be nice to get in some more construction work before winter came. There was a knock on the office door.

"Vivian!" Becky said, opening the door. "It's great to see you. I had almost forgotten that we were going to work on the next phase of the growth plan this morning." She ushered Vivian into the room. "I just got a call from a potential new customer who needs some rough-ins done."

Vivian pulled her notebook from her briefcase. "You most likely wouldn't have gotten that job."

Becky looked puzzled. "What do you mean? How do you know that?"

Vivian said, "That was me. I wanted to experience first-hand how you handle a potential new customer. We have a lot of work to do."

inquiries. At your current conversion rate of 60 percent, you would have 45 new customers.

75 inquiries X 60% conversion rate = 45 new customers

So, if we can increase the number of inquiries to 90, then we will have more customers.

90 inquiries X 60% conversion rate = 54 new customers

Definitely an improvement. However, if you do not simultaneously focus on increasing your conversion rate, you are also increasing the number of people who will *not* become customers. When you had 75 inquiries and were able to convert 45 of them into customers, you also had 30 people who telephoned your restaurant and decided to not become customers. When you start increasing the number of inquiries, you also increase the number of non-customers. We now have 36 people who will not become customers (90-54=36).

The danger of this is that people who are unsatisfied with a business tend to tell their friends and associates that they are unhappy. They might say things like, "I called the restaurant and they were really rude when I asked about vegetarian choices" or "When I called, they told me I couldn't get a reservation for another three weeks, so I called another restaurant."

The last thing that you want to be doing is increasing the number of people in your community who will never do business with you. That's why you must also focus on the second method of attracting new customers.

Increasing your conversion rate

When a potential customer calls you on the telephone, he or she will decide in the space of a few moments whether or not to buy from you. What can you do to influence his or her decision? As we've seen from the two scenarios at the beginning of the chapter, the way the telephone is answered and the information provided has a huge impact on the buy/not buy decision. Try adopting the following characteristics during any telephone (or face-to-face) interaction with potential customers:

- **Be personable.** It doesn't matter if you're having a bad day and have too much work to do. There is nothing more important for your business than speaking with a customer or potential customer, so make sure that you are not coming across as rude on the telephone. Part of being personable means that the person on the other end of the telephone feels a connection to you. Always use your name so that the customer perceives that he or she is talking to a real person who cares about his or her questions and concerns.

- **Be attentive.** True listening is a skill that every business owner and customer service provider (i.e., your employees) must learn if your business is to be successful. Take the time to truly listen to your customers, whether they are asking questions, giving praise, or voicing a complaint. Repeat back to them their concerns so it is clear that you are genuinely trying to understand what they are telling you and also to make sure that you understand them correctly.

- **Be informative.** Make sure that even the most mundane telephone conversation with your potential customers gives them more information than they were expecting. This goes back to the concept of value that we discussed in earlier chapters. Customers need to feel that they are receiving value from the businesses that they interact with. If you are providing them with useful information when they are speaking with you for the first time, it will make an impression.

- **Close the deal!** Make it clear to potential customers that you want their business. ASK for their business! Use phrases like:
  - "So, for which evening would you like a reservation?"
  - "What day would work best for you to have the no-charge consultation?"
  - "Would you like to take the rope ladder with you as well?"

Don't be shy about letting your customers know that you want the business. It makes them feel appreciated and it can be the single best strategy for increasing your revenues.

So, how does your business stack up in the area of converting potential customers into customers? As always, it's important to analyze actual numbers rather than leaving it up to "gut feel."

For the next month, track all of your interactions with potential customers, whether by telephone, trade show, or through your business's front door. This also applies to the interactions each of your employees has with potential customers. You may want to adapt the form in Sample 7 to use.

POTENTIAL CUSTOMER INTERACTION REVIEW FORM

DATE: _____

TYPE OF INQUIRY *(circle one)*:
Telephone/In-person at office/In-person other/E-mail

CUSTOMER NAME: _____

INQUIRY SPECIFICS *(check as many as apply)*:
_____ Product or service specifics
_____ Pricing
_____ Hours of operation
_____ Experience
_____ How-to information
_____ Other (please elaborate) _____

Did customer agree to buy during the interaction? *(circle one)*: YES/NO

If no, why not? _____

_____

_____

Other relevant information_____

_____

_____

Once you have tracked the interactions with your potential customers for the period of one month, you will have some good information that can help you make changes to your business. You will know how many opportunities you had to present yourself to new customers. You will also know what your potential customers ask you about. This will help you to prepare information for your employees to use in future interactions.

You will also be able to calculate an estimate of your conversion rate. Although it won't be perfect because it does not consider those customers who are only delaying their purchase instead of refusing to purchase, it will give you a good indication of how good your closing skills are.

To calculate your current customer conversion rate, simply take the number of forms on which the inquiry became a customer and divide it by the number of completed forms. For example, if you had a total of 57 filled-out forms and, of those, 22 people went on to become customers, then your conversion rate is:

$$22/57 = 39\%$$

Using Scripts

Now that we've had a look at how to handle potential customer interactions and different ways of increasing the conversion rate, you need to decide what changes you want to make in your own business. If you go back and have another look at the franchise model in Chapter 3, you'll notice that all customer interactions are scripted; that is, they have been written out and memorized. At first, you may think that this might make your business impersonal and stilted, but, in fact, it will ensure that your message comes across consistently every time someone from your business interacts with a customer or potential customer.

Develop your own telephone script by writing down your ideal telephone call: one that is interactive, friendly, and results in a sale. Refer back to the section above on the art of closing the deal to understand what to include in the script.

Once you have developed your telephone script, meet with all of your employees who have access to interactions with your customers and train them on the script. Make sure that they understand enough about your product or service to be able to help your customers, whether it be by telephone or in person.

Sample 8 is the telephone script that I had all of my team members use in my accounting practice. You can alter it to suit your own needs.

CASE STUDY

Becky said, "I guess I never really thought about how I answer the telephone. But I see now what a huge difference it makes to the customer."

"And to your bottom line," answered Vivian.

The office phone rang. Becky looked over at Vivian.

Vivian put her hands in the air. "It's not me this time. But can you put it on the speakerphone so I can hear?"

"Good morning. Joe's Plumbing. This is Becky."

"Hi, Becky. It's Mrs. Granger calling. I'm a little worried about the garbage disposal unit in my kitchen. It's making some strange noises. Do you think Joe could come out to have a look at it?"

"Thanks for calling, Mrs. Granger. Joe can certainly come out and have a look at it for you. There's a service that we provide that you might be very interested in. It's becoming very popular with customers such as yourself. It's called the Fall Maintenance Package. Joe will come out and inspect all of your visible plumbing, including the garbage disposal, to make sure that there are no blockages or leaks. He will look at the seals on the toilets to check that they're not breaking down and he will also drain your water heater. That will help to extend its life. The service costs $95 plus tax and it will give you some peace of mind knowing that everything has been looked at. Of course, if something is truly wrong with the garbage disposal, Joe will fix that while he's there. That repair will cost $40 per hour. Most garbage disposal repairs take less than two hours. Would you like to schedule a Fall Maintenance Package?"

Sample 8
TELEPHONE SCRIPT

Always answer telephone on the second ring.

Smile before you pick up the telephone (clients will hear it in your voice).

Good morning *(or afternoon)*, Mohr & Company, this is *(staff member first name, last name)*.

1. If person that the caller is looking for is available:

   Hi, *(client first name)*. Yes, she is available, I'll put you right through.

2. If person that the caller is looking for is not currently available:

   She's with someone at the moment. Is there some way that I can help?

(Assist caller as best you can. If you are unable to do so, let the caller know that you will leave a message with the staff member that the caller was originally looking for and that he or she will return the call within four business hours.)

Thanks for calling and have a great day!

CASE STUDY
continued

"Oh, that sounds wonderful. Can Joe come out tomorrow sometime?"

Becky finished scheduling the appointment and smiled at Vivian as she hung up the telephone. "How did I do?" she asked.

"Much better. You closed the deal and sold a service that the customer didn't even know about when she first called. She's clearly happy with the appointment. It's a win-win situation. And Joe most likely would have done much of that work anyway as part of the service call. This way, he's getting paid for it."

You can see how this would make clients or potential clients react. They would know with whom they are talking because the staff member would have identified himself or herself. Even if the person they were looking for wasn't available, the staff member who has picked up the telephone has asked if he or she could help the caller instead. This makes the clients feel as if the business cares above all else about their concerns and questions.

A Word about Screening Callers

"May I tell her who's calling?" This is a familiar phrase heard by customers on the telephone every day.

Many small businesses ask callers their names before they put them through to the staff member for whom they're asking. From a business's point of view, it allows the staff member to be prepared for the caller and perhaps to assemble any files or other information that he or she needs to complete the call.

From a customer's perspective, however, this tactic is viewed as a method of figuring out if the caller is worth speaking to or not. It tends to create barriers between the customer and the business, something I recommend against when trying to build a business based on trust.

Actively screening a caller is unnecessary as well. Using the telephone script above, the staff member introduces himself or herself, thereby soliciting an introduction from the caller. Even if the caller doesn't identify himself or herself, technology now allows us to know the identity of callers through Call Display. So, we have thus eliminated the business reason for screening calls.

Tracking Conversion Rate Changes

We now know how to calculate your business's conversion rate and we've looked at some methods of improving that rate. As with any other change in your business, it is important to track the changes in your conversion rate that are due to changes in the way that you do business. For example, once your telephone scripts are in place, track your conversions using the same form that you used to calculate your original conversion rate. If you notice that there are no discernible changes in the rate, try some new changes to the telephone script and test the impact of those. Continually work on improving your customer closing skills and you will notice the impact on your revenues quickly.

Chapter Summary

➡ Seemingly small changes in the way that you and your staff interact with your customers can have a huge impact on customer acquisition and retention and, therefore, revenues.

➡ The first of the three ways to grow your business, attracting new customers, can be further broken down into the activities of getting more potential customers in front of you and increasing your conversion rate from potential customer to customer.

➡ To project a consistent message to your customers, develop a telephone script to be used by every staff member who has interaction with your customers and potential customers.

➡ It's important to understand your current conversion rate and to track the changes in your conversion rate due to changes in your business model.

Checklist 10
YOUR CUSTOMER INTERACTIONS

1. I have spent time examining other companies'
    telephone procedures.   ❑

2. I have drafted a telephone script for my business
    and have documented procedures on how to handle
    telephone interactions with cutomers.   ❑

3. I know what my current customer conversion ratio is.   ❑

4. I have developed a plan to increase my business's
    conversion ratio.   ❑

5. I have provided training to my employees on
    customer interactions.   ❑

6. I actively work on my own listening skills to improve
    my customer interactions.   ❑

7. I have developed methods to ask for a customer's business. ❑

Your Marketing and Promotions

How much should you spend on trying to bring new customers in the door? In Chapter 5, we've seen that this approach is only one of three that we should be pursuing to grow your business. Yet, it's still an important one.

Many business "experts" will tell you that advertising costs should be a set percentage of your total expenses, somewhere between 3 percent and 5 percent. However, when you look at this approach more closely, you will realize that it does not make any intuitive sense. Advertising costs bear no relation to the other costs on your income statement. They are more closely related to your revenues, although this isn't always the case, either. Think about your business when you first started up. You had zero revenues and most likely a substantial advertising budget. That budget would not have changed in perfect step with the increases in revenue over time.

A more useful approach in deciding how much to spend on your advertising is to look at the lifetime value of your customers.

The Lifetime Value of a Customer

Understanding the true value of a customer assists you in managing your business. It allows you to more accurately predict your

CASE STUDY

cash flows. It also lets you know how much to spend on advertising to bring in a similar customer.

Unfortunately, very few business owners think in terms of the lifetime value of their customers. They think only about the customer's initial purchase. Some businesses make the fatal mistake of treating their customers according to how much they spend when they first come through the door: big customers get the "red carpet" treatment, and small ones get indifference. These businesses are missing a clear understanding of what that customer will bring in to the business over the long term.

The lifetime value of a customer is simply the amount of profit that the customer will add to your business over the length of the customer-supplier relationship.

Let's look at an example:

Janine owns a bottled-water company. She sells water coolers as well as five-gallon bottles of water. Her customers consist mostly of other small- and medium-size businesses that have standing orders for a set number of water bottles per week, which Janine's drivers deliver to the customers' place of business. The water coolers sell for $95, and each bottle of water sells for $5.25. Janine has calculated that her average customer purchases 2.5 bottles per week or 130 per year. The cost to Janine to purchase the water coolers is $63.50, the average cost of each bottle of water is $2.10, and the cost to deliver each bottle of water is $1.05.

When new customers come to see Janine, they usually purchase a cooler and a few bottles of water. Therefore, on the initial sale, Janine makes:

Water cooler:	**($95.00 - $63.50)**	**$31.50**
4 bottles of water: 4 @	**($5.25 - $2.10 - $1.05)**	**+ 8.40**
Total gross profit on sale:		**$39.90**

Basically, this is a $40 sale. If you were Janine, what would you spend to attract a $40 customer? Clearly less than $40. But Janine understands that this new customer is worth significantly more than that.

We know that, on average, a customer purchases 130 bottles per year. Janine has calculated that customers usually stay with her company at least three years. Therefore, the value of this customer to Janine is:

Initial sale:	$39.90
Ongoing water sales:	819.00
($2.10 gross profit per bottle X 130 bottles per year X 3 years)	
Total gross profit:	**$ 858.90**

We will ignore the impact of the time value of money for this example, but to be slightly more accurate, the total value would be a little less as tomorrow's dollars are not worth as much as today's dollars.

By this calculation, instead of this being a $40 customer, he or she is an almost $900 customer. NOW what would you spend to get this customer's business? Significantly more than $40.

Covering the Cost of the "Dry Holes"

Let's take the information that we have just learned about the lifetime value of a customer and tie it back into your growth plan.

Let's look at Janine's bottled-water company again. Janine has made some growth projections for the upcoming year. Her goal is to attract 30 new customers in the new year. We have seen that each of these new customers is worth $858.90 in profit to Janine over an average three-year period, so this translates into a three-year revenue increase of $25,767. Janine knows from experience that she can convert 65 percent of inquiries into sales. Therefore, she has calculated the required inquiries as:

30 new customers/65% = 46 inquiries

In other words, in order to reach her goal of 30 new customers next year, she needs to generate 46 inquiries through her marketing efforts. Therefore, Janine's marketing efforts have to cover the cost of 46 leads.

How would Janine know what kind of marketing effort it takes to generate 46 leads? She has tracked her former marketing campaigns. So, Janine knows, for example, that when she runs a display ad for three consecutive months in the local business magazine (at a cost of $2,250), it generates 16 leads on average. She also knows that when she runs a series of 48 radio spots (at a package cost of $7,350) during the morning drive time on the local talk radio station, it will bring in, on average, 39 calls. Janine's experience has shown her that when she runs advertising campaigns in multiple media (like print and radio), the lead generations for each go down by 10 percent as some inquiries would come in because potential customers were responding to both initiatives.

CASE STUDY

Joe looked puzzled. "So, we're going to do radio? I thought we were going to run ads in the newspaper."

Becky said, "We got a much better response from our radio ads two years ago. Vivian and I have been going over the ad copy we used and what our customer response was."

Vivian interjected, "With some changes in the copy, I think we'll get an even better response this time. We'll track the results carefully and then we can fine-tune the process for next time."

Becky said, "I can't wait to see how people respond to our new maintenance package. I think it really sets us apart from our competitors."

"That's great. Now we'll just have to make sure that I have time available to go and see all the new customers. If that's our biggest problem, I'm a pretty happy guy."

Combining the two advertising initiatives would bring in:

16 (print) + 39 (radio) - 10% = 49 leads

Janine has chosen to run both marketing initiatives simultaneously as it will generate slightly more than the 46 leads that she needs to get her 30 new customers. But is the cost worth the benefit?

Let's look at each one:

Cost

Print ads	$2,250
Radio	7,350
Total cost	$9,600

Benefit

30 customers X $858.90 =	$25,767

This tells Janine that the cost of the campaign of $9,600 is far less than the benefit she will receive of $25,767 over the average three-year lifetime of the new customers and, therefore, is beneficial for her to run.

Customers Beget Customers

The one happy complexity that we have not yet looked at is the fact that new customers will bring in more new customers. When customers are happy with your service or product, they will tell their friends and associates. In Janine's case (above), the 30 new customers that she is aiming for will most likely result in many more customers. Once you have had experience tracking your business growth, you will be able to incorporate growth due to referrals into your calculations.

This demonstrates the power of measuring and monitoring your business's historical performance. By doing so, you will be able to make marketing and growth decisions with more precision and with less cost. You will know which methods of attracting new customers work and which ones are doomed to fail. Without this knowledge, you will be doomed to repeat your failures at significant cost in time and money. Using the knowledge gives you a distinct advantage over your competitors.

Checklist 11
YOUR MARKETING AND PROMOTIONS

1. I have calculated the average lifetime value of my customer. ❑

2. I know how many leads I will have to generate to be able to attain my planned number of customers. ❑

3. I know what my historical track record has been regarding how many new customers each of my marketing initiatives has yielded. ❑

4. I have determined the optimal mix of advertising initiatives that will provide my business with the most profitable leads at the least cost. ❑

5. I have set the budget for advertising for the next 12 months. ❑

6. I have set up a plan to provide incentives to existing customers to refer new customers to my business. ❑

7. I have ensured that the advertising copy for the upcoming 12 months is in step with my company's vision and mission statements. ❑

Chapter

12

Your People

Of all the difficult processes that you will learn as a small-business owner, human resource management may be the most challenging. Not only will you have to hire, train, and (unfortunately) fire employees, you will have to learn all about the applicable labor laws in your jurisdiction, as well as payroll withholdings and taxes. Not to mention how to keep your staff happy, motivated, and productive! Once you have more than just yourself and your immediate family working in your business, there are many added complexities. However, if you want to grow your business, ultimately you will have to leverage the labor of others.

How Do You Know When It's Time to Hire?

Most small businesses begin with one person: the owner/manager. If the business is successful, customer need will eventually outstrip the time that the owner/manager has available. There are many indications that it's time for the business to hire an outside employee. However, before any hiring is done, it's critical to have all of the four foundation walls (as discussed in Chapter 1) in place. This means that, in addition to entrepreneurial drive and vision, you need to have an appropriate record keeping system, have a management operating plan in place, and know what your growth and expense projections are. Many small businesses make the mistake of hiring too early or too late because they didn't know what goals the business had and what it was looking for from a new employee.

"I have to admit," Joe said, "I'm a little nervous about hiring a plumber's apprentice. What if we don't get along with each other? And what if he screws up a job? I can't look over his shoulder all the time."

Vivian said, "Some of those issues can be dealt with in the interview process. You'll be able to get a good idea about how he or she operates. You've already done the projections and you know that hiring someone skilled is essential to your growth plan."

"I know. We've just never had any experience with employees before. I don't know how to go about it."

Vivian said, "Let's start with the basics."

Once you have the basics in place, there are several "road markers" that you can look out for that will tell you that it's time to start looking for an employee:

- Your revenues would increase by more than the additional payroll expense if you were able to concentrate on your strengths.

- You are unable to spend at least 20 percent of your time working *on* your business in the planning and strategizing activities.

- You do not have the time to implement the marketing and promotion plan that's required to achieve your projected growth.

- You are approaching your capacity with regards to labor inputs (i.e., your projected sales will require more hours than are physically possible).

- You are spending money on late fees and penalties because you cannot stay on top of the accounts payable and the required government filings.

- You begin to feel tired and "burned out" all of the time. You will notice the impact of this state fairly quickly as your productivity will decline drastically.

Any one of these indicators requires that you spend some time considering additional staff. Before you hire, however, you will have to decide what you need that person to do.

What Will a New Employee Do?

There are many different ways to decide what you want your new employee or employees to do. It could be that they look after the things that you're not getting around to doing, or the things that you're not very good at or that you don't like doing.

The first step in making that decision is to outline all the "jobs" in your business. You may not have thought about your business as having several different jobs because you are the only one doing them. It may all seem like one super-sized job to you. Separating out the functions, however, will help you to decide what needs to be done.

Jobs are simply a collection of processes. In previous chapters, we have changed, deleted, and added processes as we have built our business machine. These processes can be grouped into natural clusters to form an employee's job responsibilities. Some of the common processes are:

- Accounts receivable (billing, collection, tracking, cash handling)
- Accounts payable (tracking, check production)
- Office support (answering calls, greeting customers, booking appointments, filing, making coffee)
- Sales (customer presentations, follow-up, cold-calling, trade shows)
- Marketing and promotion (managing advertising, marketing tools design, writing copy, customer letters)
- Production (running the equipment, providing services to customers)
- Operations management (overseeing the production process, supervising employees, operational reporting)

Once you have outlined what the processes are in your business, it's time to document them. This will clarify for you and your employee what the expectations of the job are. Sample 9 is a sample documentation of the accounts receivable process in a small pest control company. You can modify and customize as you need to create your own template.

In a small business, this process likely would not take enough time to be a full job. It would be combined with other processes to form an employee's workload.

Once you have outlined all the processes in your business, take some time to honestly assess your own strengths and weaknesses. Are you good at sales but not so good at bookkeeping? Are you skilled at putting together a detailed budget but not at handling customer complaints? The goal here is to give yourself the set of processes where you add the most value, and hire someone to do a great job at the processes where you are the weakest.

The Laws of the Land

Now you know what skill set you are looking for. Great! But before you place that first ad for a new employee, it's important to understand your rights and responsibilities as an employer. These rules will be different in every jurisdiction so make sure that your information is correct. Call your local government office or speak with your accountant about it. This will save you considerable grief in the future.

Sample 9
DOCUMENTING YOUR WORK PROCESSES

BeGone Pest Control Inc.
Process Documentation

Process name: Accounts receivable

Process goals: To bill customers and collect monies owed in a timely manner. To minimize bad debts and to maximize customer good will.

Process tasks:

Bill customer for services rendered within one business day.

Send statements of account to all customers who have outstanding accounts at the end of every calendar month. Statements will be sent by the fifth of the following month.

Telephone all customers who have accounts outstanding for 45 days to request payment.

Send final notice statements of account to all customers who have outstanding accounts for 60 days.

Liaise with the collection agency regarding delinquent accounts.

Process receipts and update accounting system the day of the receipt.

Most jurisdictions have rules on the following topics:
- The type of workplace that you must provide for an employee
- The minimum wage you can pay
- How hazardous materials with which the employee comes into contact must be stored
- How much paid vacation time and sick days an employee is entitled to
- What deductions you must withhold from an employee's paycheck and remit to the government
- How maternity leaves are to be handled by the employer
- Under what circumstances you can fire an employee and how much notice he or she is to be given

There may be dozens of other rules that you must follow, so make sure you get a handle on them before hiring.

Attracting Quality Employees

Now you're ready to advertise for your first employee. You know what you want the employee to do and you know what skill set you are looking for. But how can you express that in an ad? And how do you make your ad more attractive to potential candidates than those of your competitors?

Your ad will have several considerations:

1. **The job description.** Have a clearly worded description so that candidates get a good sense right away what's involved in the job and whether they have the requisite skills.

2. **The business description.** Describe your business and its industry.

3. **The requirements.** Here's where you tell the candidates what they need to have in the way of education, experience, or technical skills. Be as clear as possible so that you do not have to wade through dozens of resumes with unsuitable qualifications.

4. **Contact information.** Describe how the candidates should respond to the ad: by telephone, fax, email, or in person. Including this information will save you from unwanted interruptions in your business day. It can also pick out unsuitable candidates right away. For example, if your ad states that potential candidates should fax their resume and three people show up in person, it tells you that these three might not be very good at following rules. In some positions, this might be a plus, but in most situations, this can be a negative quality.

5. **Tone.** The tone of your ad is difficult to quantify but it tells potential employees a lot about your business and the workplace environment. For example, if your environment is casual and laid back, you will want to convey that by using an informal tone in your ad, which will let candidates know up front whether or not that is the environment they want to work in.

Sample 10 is an actual employment ad that I ran in my own accounting firm.

EMPLOYMENT ADVERTISEMENT

Create Beans,
don't just count them!

If you want to be a key team member in a fast-paced, fun, and different kind of accounting firm, then we want to hear from you!

Our new Director of Compliance Services will have the following skills:

- The ability to provide top-notch client service
- Outstanding, proven leadership skills
- Experience in an accounting firm
- Above-average computer skills
- A positive, upbeat attitude

The **REWARDS** are many!

- Above-average compensation
- A dynamic, exciting work environment
- The ability to shape your own career
- A performance-based bonus structure

Please send resume along with cover letter to:

Mohr & Company
1111 Any Street
Anytown, Anyprovince T0T 0T0

Think of your ad as a way to present your business to highly skilled, motivated potential employees. Remember that your customers will also read your ad. They will get a strong sense of the quality of your staff from what you are asking for in the ad, so make sure that your ad exudes professionalism and demands the same from employees.

Once you have a number of resumes in front of you, it's time to narrow the playing field. Start by removing any candidate who does not have the background or skills asked for in the ad (I will guarantee that you will get some of those, especially in a tough job market). Have a look at the remaining resumes. Are there candidates who are clearly more qualified than others? Is there someone who claims to have outstanding attention to detail but who misspells several words in the cover letter? Is there someone with important skills that you did not even consider when placing the ad?

Narrow your field to a half dozen candidates or less. You will want to interview several people as you are also honing your hiring skills. You want as much experience as possible at the task.

The Interview

It's now time to talk to your potential candidates. There are many theories on the interview process, and it would be a good idea to pick up a good book on interviewing skills.

The purpose of the interview is for the candidate and the employer to find out enough information to assess whether this would be a good job fit. Never forget that the candidate will be interviewing you too. Ensure that you are prepared and professional — the same qualities you are looking for in an employee.

It's best to have your interview questions prepared ahead of time. That way, you'll know that you've asked everything you meant to and you will be able to compare answers among candidates.

During the interview, talk to the candidate about your business. Tell him or her about how you've systematized processes and about your growth plans for the future. An appropriate candidate will be interested in learning more about your business.

Ultimately, you will make your decision based on a combination of factors, including the answers to your questions, professional image, enthusiasm, salary expectations, and "gut feel." As you become more experienced in human resource management, your instincts will be sharper and more valuable to you.

Hiring from an Employment Agency

With strict labor laws in most industrialized countries, it can be very difficult to let an employee go once he or she has been hired on a permanent basis. There is also great expense to the employer of hiring and training an employee who doesn't work out, never mind the stress of firing someone.

That's why many employers hire temporary employees and it can be a valuable strategy for small-business owners. Many employment agencies hire out workers on a weekly or monthly basis to businesses that have variable staffing needs. For example, if your busy time is at Christmas and you need help to fill orders over the holiday season, you may wish to hire someone on a temporary basis. At the end of the contract, the employee goes back to the agency to be hired by some other business.

Hiring a temporary employee has some benefits for you if you are hiring your first employee:

- The agency has already performed much of the pre-screening.

- You will get a better sense of what you are looking for in an employee once you have one.

- If the person doesn't work out or you find out that you don't have enough work to keep him or her busy, you can send the employee back to the agency at the end of the contract, without the challenges surrounding firing a permanent employee.

- If the employee and your business end up being a match made in heaven, you can hire the employee on a permanent basis. (The agency may have some rules about that, so make sure you find out what they are ahead of time).

- Hiring a temporary employee can be a great way to "get your feet wet" in the human resource area.

Goal-Based Compensation

Once you have gotten through the jungle of defining roles, advertising, interviewing, and hiring a new employee, you may think that it's time to put your feet up and take a breather. But not so! (You knew I was going to say that.) A more difficult challenge than hiring a great employee is keeping a great employee. Lots of businesses are looking for skilled labor. You are in competition not only with other businesses in your industry but with all other businesses in your area. Savvy workers will continually be looking for better opportunities with more pay and greater benefits. It is your responsibility to make sure not only that the employee is a good fit with your business, but also that he or she is motivated and happy to come to work everyday. These are skills that you need to learn to be successful, but which are outside the scope of this book. For more information on human resource management, check out *The HR Book*, another title in the Self-Counsel series.

One valuable facet of managing employees is to make sure that they are compensated to do the things that you want them to do. This ensures that the performance of the employees is in sync with the goals of your business. For example, if employees have control over the sales function, make part of their compensation based on sales growth, not expense reduction. Reward them for furthering the vision of the business and let them participate in the strategic outlook. The second book in the *Numbers 101 for Small Business* series, *Financial Management 101*, has a chapter dedicated to employee compensation.

So Long, Farewell, Auf Wiedersehen, Adieu

One of the hardest tasks you will ever perform as an employer is to have to fire someone. Not only is it disruptive from an operations standpoint, but it also has implications on personal relationships and finances. How would you feel if you had to fire a single mother and remove her only source of income?

The best way to avoid this is to spend considerable time and effort in the hiring process. It's also critical to give feedback in the employee evaluation process so that you are both "on the same page" regarding expectations and obstacles. Sometimes, however, an employment situation just doesn't work out no matter how hard both parties have tried. How do you know it's time to let someone go? Here are some signs:

- Negative customer feedback
- Tension with other employees
- A significant reduction in productivity
- Inability to complete job functions without constant supervision and prodding
- Declining morale in the office

Any one of these signs can be due to a number of factors, so it is only after you have discussed the problems with the employee and have given him or her an opportunity to fix them that you

CASE STUDY

Becky shuffled through the pile of resumes and looked up at Vivian. "Well, we got 17 resumes and we interviewed 5 candidates."

Vivian asked, "And did you and Joe come to a decision?"

"Yeah," Joe said. "We both agreed on Martin. Before we interviewed him, I didn't think that he'd be the one. But he's got all the skills and he's worked for a plumber before, so he's got experience. And he seems easy to get along with."

"Now we just have to keep him!" Becky said.

Chapter Summary

→ You'll know it's time to hire an employee when the increased revenues due to having an employee more than offset the increased payroll expense, allowing you to focus on your strengths.

→ Have a detailed description of all your internal processes and an accurate assessment of your own strengths and weaknesses before you decide what skills and background you require from potential candidates.

→ It may be beneficial to hire on a temporary basis your first time to get a better idea of what you're really looking for.

→ Waiting too long to fire someone who is a bad fit can have serious repercussions on the morale of the business.

should consider termination. You will also have to be familiar with employment law in your jurisdiction so that you do not end up looking at the business end of a wrongful termination lawsuit.

There are costs involved in hiring, training, supervising, and firing employees. How you handle these activities can have an impact on your bottom line, so take the time to do it right.

Checklist 12
YOUR PEOPLE

1. I have calculated whether my projected increase in revenues from hiring an employee will outweigh the cost. ❑

2. I have reviewed whether I am still able to spend at least 20 percent of my working time on planning and strategizing activities. ❑

3. I have outlined all the jobs in my business. ❑

4. I have clustered all the jobs in my business into natural clusters to form employees' job responsibilities. ❑

5. I have prepared complete documentation for every procedure in the business. ❑

6. I have educated myself regarding the employment laws in my jurisdiction. ❑

7. I have written an employment ad that encompasses not only the specific job responsibilities, but also the nature of the working environment. ❑

8. I have considered hiring a temporary employee. ❑

9. I have documented the employment contract and the basis of compensation. ❑

Chapter 13

Your Systems

So far, we have looked at making changes in our business in order to grow successfully: changes in our marketing approach, our human resource policies, and the way we interact with customers.

Now it's time to bring all of the new ways of doing things together to make a cohesive guidebook for your business.

The Goals of Systemization

The goal of growing your business is to increase profits and ultimately increase the value of the business in order to sell it. The reason a systems approach works is that it allows you, the owner and manager of the business, to repeat processes and procedures in a predictable and consistent way. It also allows you to train your staff to perform these functions exactly the same way that you would. Not only does this give customers a consistent buying experience, but it also makes it easier for staff to learn new tasks and feel confident that they are doing things the right way (i.e., the way you want them to do it).

In the second book in the *Numbers 101 for Small Business* series, *Financial Management 101*, we learned how to develop a management operating plan. This is a tool for you as the owner and manager of your business to track critical business processes such as the following topics:

- Team meeting agendas and minutes
- Key performance indicators

CASE STUDY

"It's hard to believe that everything we do is in that binder," Becky said, leafing through the new Joe's Plumbing procedures manual.

Joe added, "Yeah. It's not so long ago that we didn't even know what we were doing, never mind being able to write it down in a way that makes sense."

"It makes our company feel more permanent somehow. Like it's going to outlast us," said Becky.

"The real test will come soon when the new apprentice reads it over. Then we'll know whether it makes sense to anyone else."

"That's the most detailed "how to" guide I've ever seen," said Martin. "Everything's in here. Why we do things, how to do them, everything."

Becky said, "Take some time to read it over carefully. We've put a lot of effort into creating systems for this company so that it will run more smoothly."

Martin said, "Well, I look forward to working here. You're certainly a lot more organized than the last place I worked."

Joe and Becky laughed and smiled at each other, remembering the not too distant past where organization didn't even seem possible.

- Historical financial statements
- Budgets and cash flow projections

Documentation of your systems will form a part of this management operating plan. In my accounting firm, we called this, "How We Do It Here," which is pretty self-explanatory.

"How We Do It Here"

Your process and procedure manual (whatever you choose to call it) should start with your business's vision and mission statements. These are the first things a new employee needs to know about your business: its guiding principles and focus. The principles in the vision and mission statements form the underlying basis for every procedure and every customer interaction.

Knowing these principles will also allow employees to identify areas where the procedures do not further the goals of the organization. In this way, the employees will ensure that the manual is continually reviewed and fine-tuned.

After the vision and mission statements, include a section on your human resource policy. There will be many parts to this (an example follows in Sample 11 at the end of this chapter). In this section, you will cover the following issues:

- Hours of work
- Vacation and sick leave
- Dress code
- Overtime policy
- Performance evaluation process
- Reporting structure

There may be other issues important to your business that you wish to include. The purpose of this section is to give employees a clear sense of your expectations of them. This will serve you well as it provides an objective starting point from which to discuss any performance problems in the future.

Following the human resource section, you can include your procedure documentation, grouped by process. For example, in your marketing section (a process), you might have a sheet for advertising policies, one for trade show procedures, and one for how referrals are generated and handled.

The procedural documentation should be specific and clear. To test that this is the case, have a new employee read the documentation for a particular procedure and see if he or she can perform the task based on the manual. Anything that you have to explain should be incorporated into the documentation. The goal is to make training easy and consistent, with a minimum amount of your time.

Continuous Improvement

Like all areas of your business, the systems you develop will be constantly refined, tested, and fine-tuned.

For example, you may have discovered that the telephone script you are currently using converts 62 percent of inquiries into sales. Test a new script to see if does better. Change the headlines that you use in your print advertising and test whether the new one generates more leads than the old one. By making sure that your business is fresh and growing, you can help defer the decline stage of your business's life cycle.

As new processes are developed and old ones become obsolete, make sure that you update your operations manual. If you have employees, assign the updating responsibility to one of them. That will ensure that it actually gets done.

Developing and refining the systems in your business will set you apart from your competitors. Take the time to do it right!

Sample 11 is an excerpt from the policy manual from my own company. You can use it as a starting point for developing your own policy manual to document your systems approach.

Chapter Summary

➡ Having systems in your business allows you and your employees to operate in a repeatable, consistent fashion.

➡ Having a process and procedures manual as part of your monthly operating plan conveys "the way we do it here" to all employees, which gives you greater freedom from having to supervise.

➡ A process and procedures manual contains documentation on the business's vision and mission statements, human resource policies, and operational procedures.

➡ Systems should be frequently revised and tested to continuously improve your business, and the procedures manual should be updated to reflect any changes.

Sample 11
HUMAN RESOURCE POLICY

(Excerpt from the Mohr & Company policy manual)

HOW WE DO IT HERE
Our Team's Commitment to Each Other

1. Each team member will treat other team members with respect and professionalism.

2. Team members will ensure that any concerns or issues they may have are raised with the appropriate person or the managing partner.

3. All team members deserve to know how they are performing and semi-annual performance appraisal reviews (PARS) will be held with each team member and his or her manager. Input on performance will be solicited from all members of the team.

4. Each team member plays an integral role in the success of the firm. Therefore, every person has a responsibility to provide input on making the team and the firm better. All suggestions and recommendations will be taken seriously by all team members and discussed.

5. Each team member should realize that the goal of the firm is to get all work done in a timely manner. Team members should recognize situations where they might be able to help another team member with a task, and the team should discuss resource allocation of the firm as a whole.

Working Hours

The office is generally open from 9 until 5 Monday to Friday and there must be at least one staff member present in the office at all times. Keeping this general rule in mind, team members may exercise their own judgment in planning their working hours, remembering that the needs of the clients supersede this flexibility.

Our standard work week is 37.5 hours and any hours worked in excess of the standard can be "banked" and used as time off in the future.

Employees will receive two weeks of paid vacation, the timing of which will be discussed and approved by the entire team.

Sample 11 — Continued

Employees will be paid for a maximum of six sick days during a calendar year. Any sick days in excess of this will be deducted from the team member's pay. Family emergencies (the illness of a child, for example) can be taken as part of the paid sick leave.

Internet and E-Mail Use Policy

The internet and e-mail access is primarily for company use. Uses of internet and e-mail include accounting and tax research, downloading of government forms, and correspondence with clients and other team members.

It is understood that some personal transactions are most easily handled on the internet, such as web banking. These types of personal uses are acceptable as long as the time taken is minimal. Excessive internet browsing for personal purposes should be done at home.

Under no circumstances should any information or document of any kind be downloaded from the internet unless approved by the partners. Downloading can expose the network to malicious viruses. The partners can provide you with a list of "safe" websites from which it is low risk to download information.

Your e-mail address, yourname@mohrandcompany.com, exists for the purpose of contacting and conversing with clients and team members. Personal e-mail should not be sent or received from this e-mail address. You may wish to set up a free e-mail account through MSN®, Yahoo!®, etc., for the purpose of personal correspondence, and you may check this account periodically as per the internet use rules above.

Dress Code

All team members should dress professionally at the office. The dress code is "business casual." For men, this means well-pressed pants and either a dress shirt or golf shirt. For women, this means a well-pressed skirt or pants and a blouse, dress shirt, or golf shirt.

As an alternative, team members can wear tan or black dress pants and shirts with the company logo.

Team members should be aware that there may be times when more formal dress is appropriate.

Checklist 13
YOUR SYSTEMS

1. I have reviewed all processes and procedures in my business to make sure that they are efficient and relevant. ❑

2. I have prepared a complete process and procedure manual for my company on planning and strategizing activities. ❑

3. I have prepared a training and professional development program for all my employees. ❑

4. All my employees have read the company's vision and mission statements and understand them. ❑

5. All my employees are thoroughly trained on all their job responsibilities. ❑

6. All my employees have read and understand the company's human resource policies. ❑

7. I have set up a system to continuously monitor and measure my company's systems. ❑

Chapter

14

Business Acquisitions

So far in this book, we have discussed growing your business organically, by building a customer base from the ground up and using customer attraction and retention strategies.

There is another method of growth, however: buying customers. This can be accomplished in one of three ways:

- Buying a group of customers from another business
- Buying a business solely for its customer list
- Buying a business to run separately from your existing business

Regardless of which method you use, there are several issues to be considered when buying customers, including quality assessment, valuation, and infrastructure changes. Growing your business by purchasing another business can give you instant rewards, but only if managed in a planned, consistent way.

Another Way to Grow

There are many reasons why you might choose to purchase a business rather than develop your own customer base. These may include:

- High initial investment in capital equipment or staff. In some businesses that use specialized equipment in the manufacturing process, the high upfront investment needs to be recovered quickly in order to stay afloat. In this situation, it would make sense to build the customer base as quickly as possible to reach capacity in order to offset the high fixed costs. An example would be a print shop. The printing and lithography equipment is quite expensive so it would make sense to purchase the customers of another print shop to generate revenues quickly.

- Low barriers for "copycat" competitors. Sometimes, being the first out of the gate ensures that your business will be successful. Therefore, you need a full customer roster before other businesses get the same idea. An example would be if an entrepreneur opens the first paralegal service in town. Competitors would quickly see the benefits of starting up this type of company, so it makes sense for the entrepreneur to quickly ramp up to capacity (i.e., have lots of customers) before the competition get wind of the new business and try to build a customer base of their own.

- A desire to step into a successful turnkey system. Some entrepreneurs want to take advantage of a system that is guaranteed to work because the business has a great track record (remember that this is also how you want potential purchasers to feel about your business someday).

- The ability to sell to the new block of customers your complementary service or product. You may have a product or service that would almost automatically sell to a group of customers. For example, if you purchase a hairdressing salon, there's a good chance that those customers would be very interested in the spa services that your business provides (and vice versa).

What Are You Buying?

So how can you tell if a potential business acquisition is a good idea?

First, make sure you understand what you are purchasing. There are two main ways of buying a business: asset purchase and share purchase. Each has its own considerations. It is critical that you engage the services of an experienced lawyer and accountant before negotiating any business acquisition.

As well, when you buy the shares of a business, you are also buying its goodwill and customer lists.

Asset purchase

In an asset purchase, you are only buying certain assets of the business. In most situations, you will not be responsible for the debts or dealings that the business engaged in prior to the purchase. For example, you may be purchasing equipment, raw materials, inventory, or a customer list.

In some situations, you may be purchasing the net assets of the business, which means that you will be assuming responsibility for the liabilities as well. In this case, you would need to obtain legal comfort regarding the extent and terms of the liabilities. You wouldn't want, for example, to purchase the net assets of a business only to find out later that the equipment loan is due in 30 days and is $10,000 more than you thought.

Share purchase

You may also purchase the shares of a business. This basically transfers the rights and responsibilities of the ownership of the business from the seller to you. You would now own everything that the business owns, including assets, corporate information, and the business names and logos.

You would also have complete liability for the past dealings of the business, including any lawsuits, warranties, or debts as well as any back taxes owing to the government. Some of this liability can be reduced or removed through provisions in the purchase contract. You might include a clause that says that you can seek compensation from the seller for any former liabilities. This would still leave you in a position to have to settle up first and try to recover later, which could seriously disrupt your operations and cash flow.

There are, however, some benefits to purchasing the entire business through a share purchase. There are tax benefits in many jurisdictions, but, more important, you own all the goodwill that the former business has generated, as well as the business's current customer list.

Goodwill

When you buy a business, you are also buying its goodwill. Goodwill is difficult to pin down. It is an asset of the business (sometimes the most important one) but it does not have substance like manufacturing equipment or desks or raw materials. There are many accounting and legal definitions, but we are speaking here in the general sense of the word. Goodwill refers to the ability of the business to attract and retain customers. You can also define it as the business's reputation. That reputation might have been built on many platforms, which can include:

- High community profile
- Charitable donations
- Customer service
- Quality of product or service
- Treatment of employees

Buying goodwill can be a huge benefit to you as customers will come to see you because of the former activities of the business. Of course, you can always destroy that goodwill by operating the business differently than the previous owners.

In most purchase situations where the business involved has built up goodwill, the purchase price will reflect that. Therefore, the cost to you will generally be more than the value of the hard assets (we will discuss valuation later on in the chapter).

Customer lists

A customer list is almost as difficult to define as goodwill. You can't touch it or see it, but it is a valuable asset, nonetheless. A customer list simply refers to the data base of current and former customer names, addresses, and other contact information. The value of a customer list lies in marketing. It is always easier and less expensive to market to an existing customer than to attract a new customer.

For example, if you are considering purchasing a bed and breakfast in Vermont, you would (all other things being equal) be willing to pay more for one that has tracked its customers over the years and knows who they are and how many times they have stayed in the bed and breakfast. Having this information would allow you to send letters to these former guests, updating them on the happenings of the bed and breakfast and offering them special discounts or packages.

In Chapter 6, we looked at the importance of tracking customers and their buying patterns. These same principles apply to purchasing a business; it's worth more if you have a marketable customer base.

Valuing the Acquisition

Business valuation lies somewhere between a science and an art. There are dozens of books on the subject and several professional designations. The theory and application of business valuation is beyond the scope of this book, but we can look at some general considerations and some parameters.

What would you pay to buy a business? Well, the least amount that the business is worth is the liquidation value of its net assets. Let's look at a potential business purchase example. The business is a bed and breakfast, a century home in a tourist district where people can book rooms that entitle them to breakfast the next morning. The business has provided you with the information outlined in Sample 12.

How much would you pay for this business? That may be a difficult and subjective decision but at least we can put some parameters around it.

Sample 12
VALUING A BUSINESS ACQUISITION

PARADISE GARDENS B&B FINANCIAL INFORMATION

Assets: Fair market value (FMV)

House and land	$347,000
Furnishings	29,350
In-house equipment (fridge/stove/washer/dryer)	3,210
Outside equipment (lawn mower/tiller/hand tools)	1,425

Liabilities

Mortgage	$276,349
Line of credit	23,000
Property taxes in arrears	4,250

Other information

- B&B has maintained an 80 percent occupancy rate for the past six years.
- Fully rented, the B&B generates $93,075 from its three rooms.
- Operating expenses (including one maid) average $57,215 annually.
- 75 percent of customers have booked a room more than once.

Floor price

Floor price means the absolute minimum that we would pay for the business. If we look at it from a common sense perspective, we could buy the business today and sell the assets and settle the liabilities tomorrow.

Therefore, the least that the business is worth is the fair market value of its hard assets (i.e., those that you can see or touch) minus the settlement value of the liabilities. In this case, the total market value of the assets is $380,985. From that amount, we would have to settle up total liabilities of $303,599, leaving us with $77,386 in our pockets. Therefore, we would at least be willing to pay $77,386 for the business because we know that we can easily get that back out of the business.

But we also know that the fact that we already have a steady stream of customers is worth something as well. It won't take much effort on our part to maintain the 80 percent occupancy rate. The business already has made a name for itself and people are willing to come back time and time again. We're not starting this business with three empty rooms that we quickly need to fill if we're going to cover our fixed costs.

We know that, if we experience the same occupancy rate and the same operating expenses as the former owners, we will make $17,245 annually right out of the gate. So, in a sense, on top of purchasing the net assets of the business, we are also purchasing a stream of profit. The art and science of business valuation is to determine how much that stream of profit is worth to a purchaser.

Ceiling price

The ceiling price refers to the maximum we would pay for a business. In this case, we know that it will be more than the $77,386 floor price.

It will be important to make sure that we can recover our investment in a reasonable time frame. For example, if we pay $100,000 for this business, it will take almost six years to achieve payback (for a fuller discussion of payback, please refer to the second book in the *Numbers 101 for Small Business* series, *Financial Management 101*). This may or may not be a reasonable amount of time depending on your goals and income requirements.

The payback concept becomes more critical when evaluating your options.

Evaluating the Choices

If you have the option of choosing among several purchase possibilities, you need to choose one that best meets your goals. Earlier in the chapter, we talked about the reasons entrepreneurs buy a business, and some of the intangible benefits may well come into play in your decision.

From a strictly numbers standpoint, the best choice is the business that generates the most profit for the least investment. For example, if two businesses cost $50,000 each to buy and one generates $10,000 in profit annually and the other generates $14,000, clearly the second option provides the higher profit for the same money (a "bigger bang for the buck," so to speak).

On top of this basic decision model, however, you will have to factor in what other financial benefits you will receive from each purchase. If one of the businesses has customers to whom you can sell your existing products, this will be a better choice than a business that will stand alone and with which there will not be any opportunity to cross sell.

With the help of your business advisors, you'll need to weigh the financial pros and cons of each choice against each other to determine which is the better buy.

Chapter Summary

- Buying a business rather than growing one from scratch can offer several benefits, including an immediate profit stream, a recognizable brand name, or a marketable customer list.

- You can buy a business by either buying the assets of the business or by buying shares.

- Buying shares allows you to retain the goodwill that the business has built over time.

- In order to evaluate and value a potential business purchase, you need to weigh all of the financial advantages you will generate from the purchase.

Checklist 14
BUSINESS ACQUISITIONS

1. I have investigated the possibility and attractiveness of purchasing a group of customers from another business. ☐

2. I have investigated the possibility and attractiveness of buying another business solely for its customer list. ☐

3. I have investigated the possibility and attractiveness of buying another business to run in addition to my current business. ☐

4. I have investigated all of the costs and benefits of purchasing a company's shares versus buying its assets. ☐

5. I can calculate the value of a business's goodwill. ☐

6. I know how to calculate a basic valuation range for a potential business acquisition. ☐

7. I know what the comparative risks are for each of my potential purchases. ☐

Chapter

15

Exit Strategies

It may seem very strange to you to be thinking about leaving your business when you put so much effort into starting it up and growing it. But there will come a time when you will want to move on, and the earlier you plan for that eventuality, the better off you will be. Even if you plan on working until you drop, you will indeed drop someday and you need to have planned out what happens to the business then.

Many exit strategies require months or years to implement, so it makes sense to map out the strategy that's best for you as early as possible.

Your Personal Goals

In Chapter 5, we looked at your business goals in order to put together a growth plan. Now we need to review your personal goals. Ask yourself: What do you want to do after running your business?

The answers to that question are as unique as each entrepreneur. You may decide that there's nothing more appealing than lying on a faraway beach sipping margaritas. You may want to start another business, perhaps in a different industry. You may choose to mentor young entrepreneurs as they face the same pitfalls you have over the years. It's important to define your goals because they will affect how you will transfer your business and how you will structure payments.

Heading for the Exits

There are many ways to transfer your business to others. Let's look at the most common.

Passing on the business to your children

One common way to transfer your business is to pass it on to your children, which is also known as succession planning. Many small-business owners want to keep the business empire that they have created in the family to provide their children (or grandchildren) with a secure source of income. However, this form of selling the business can be the most difficult.

The first decision that has to be made is whether your children are truly interested in owning the business. Many small business owners get quite the shock to find out that their kids really don't want all the hassles of running a business. Even if they do want to take over the reigns, they must go through the same decision process as you did when you started your business: defining business and personal goals, outlining a vision, and setting a growth plan.

A decision that you as the business owner must make is to define what is acceptable to you in how the business is run in the future. What if your children have a very different vision of the business and make substantial changes? Will you be comfortable with that? The more thought put into this type of succession upfront, the more likely the transition will be successful.

Selling the business to an outside party

If you don't have a family member who wants to take on the business, you may choose to sell your business to someone outside your family. It might be an employee, a competitor, or someone who wishes to purchase an existing business rather than start one from scratch (in which case, they will assess your business in the ways we discussed in Chapter 14).

It is more difficult to sell a business than you might think. That's why it's critical to plan ahead so that you can make sure that your business looks great on paper, is growing consistently, and will be attractive to potential buyers.

Brokers are frequently used in this type of sale. A broker's job is to match up buyers and sellers of businesses, much like a real estate broker's job is to match up buyers and sellers of houses. A broker may bring potential purchasers to the table whom you may not have otherwise met.

When selling to an outside buyer, timing is important. Ideally, you will want to sell your business when the economy is hot, your business's performance looks outstanding, and its reputation is stellar. The worst thing that you can do as a small business owner is to run your business until you can't stand it for another five minutes and then try to dump it for whatever you can get. You'll maximize the business's value (and price tag) if you sell when things are looking up rather than down.

Liquidating your business

If you have built a business that is completely dependent upon you and have not systematized your operations, liquidation of the business is probably your only option. Liquidation involves selling off the assets of the business and using those funds to pay the liabilities, which will only work if there are more assets in the business than liabilities. If the situation is reversed (i.e., there are more liabilities than assets), you may have to declare bankruptcy in order to get out of your business, otherwise you will have to continue to run it until the liabilities are paid.

The benefit of liquidation is that it tends to be easier than selling a business as a going concern. There are more potential buyers for individual assets than for an entire operation. The down side (and it's a big one!) is that you will almost always end up with less cash in your pocket at the end of the day by liquidating. There are two reasons for this:

- Equipment and other assets are generally valued higher if they are part of a continuing business.
- It is impossible to sell the goodwill of your business if you are liquidating.

Generally, liquidation is the least favorable option for you to pursue.

What's My Business Worth?

In Chapter 14, we talked about business valuation from the perspective of you, the buyer. All of those issues apply here when you are looking to put a price tag on your business. You know that your business is worth at least the fair market value of the assets minus the payout value of the liabilities. If you have been working to systematize and grow your business, it will be worth substantially more.

It is worth discussing your particular situation with a business valuator. (Your accountant or lawyer should be able to recommend one.) Undervaluing your business can have serious consequences on your retirement lifestyle, so it pays to do your homework and get professional help.

Getting Ready for the Sale

There are many things that you will have to do before putting any exit strategy in place, especially if you will be selling to outside buyers.

The first thing is to assemble your team of experts. This will most likely include your accountant, lawyer, financial planner, and perhaps a business valuator and broker. Make sure that all parties know your goals for the buyout and that they are all working in tandem to meet those goals.

Your accountant will help you steer through all your choices surrounding how to structure the sale and how to take payment. There will be practical decisions as well as taxation implications.

Your lawyer will help you structure the legal side of the sale and will help you interpret offers as they come in.

Your financial planner will look at your post-business goals and will help you determine what income level you will need in order to maintain your desired lifestyle (margaritas can get expensive!). We've already discussed the roles of the business valuator and the broker. They can be integral parts of your team.

Your accountant will most likely recommend that you prepare some financial information for the pending sale. Much like a real estate broker would suggest to you that you put a fresh coat of paint on your house and maybe plant some flowers outside before bringing buyers through, your accountant will recommend that you show potential buyers of your business what it might look like once they take over. You will have run your business in a way that suited you. You may have had the goal of minimizing tax or employing your family. These decisions might not be made the same way by the new owner.

Your accountant will get you to normalize your financial statements; in other words, recast them without all of the discretionary activity. If your spouse is on the payroll, remove the expense related to that. If you pay yourself high dividends, restate the financials without them. Keep in mind, however, that you need to be upfront with potential buyers about the changes you have made and how those statements differ from ones you have prepared for taxation purposes.

The Mechanics of the Sale

A sale can happen in one of two basic ways:

- Through the sale of assets
- Through the sale of shares

If your business is unincorporated, you will be selling the assets of the business. The buyer may choose to take on some or all of the business's liabilities rather than coming up with a lot of cash upfront. Your lawyer will ensure that your name is removed from those liabilities so that creditors cannot come after you later if the new owner stops paying them.

If you own a corporation, you can either sell the assets of the business or the shares of the corporation. Each has its own tax consequences and your accountant will help you weigh the pros and cons of each. If you are passing on your business to your children, there are many sophisticated ways to transfer shares and your accountant will advise you on the various methods. You may choose to structure the arrangement, for example, so that you are still a shareholder (albeit one who no longer works in the business) and will receive a monthly income for the rest of your life in the form of dividends.

Once you and a buyer agree on the nature of the sale, you must decide how you will receive the funds: either all upfront or over time. Again, tax considerations come in to play here, but you must also consider the risk of financing part of the sale. If, for example, you agree to receive $50,000 upfront and $5,000 a month for 12 months, you are betting the farm on the fact that the new owner will still be in business a year from now. What if he or she runs the business into the ground? Or declares bankruptcy? You will lose some or all of the sales proceeds and may find yourself having to start up another business rather than lying on the beach. Your lawyer can help mitigate some of that risk through the structuring of the agreement.

Once the business has been sold, financial planning becomes a key issue, especially if you plan to retire. You are now dealing with a fixed amount of funds (which can grow through prudent investing) and you and your financial planner will have to make sure those funds plus your other sources of savings will last you for the rest of your life.

Chapter Summary

➡ It's critical to set up your exit strategy early to make sure that you will ultimately harvest the most value from the business.

➡ You may choose to pass your business onto the next generation, sell it to a third party, or sell off the assets and wind up operations.

➡ The timing of the sale can have a significant impact on the price you ultimately receive.

➡ If your business is a corporation, you can either sell the assets of the business or sell the shares of the corporation.

Checklist 15
EXIT STRATEGIES

1. I know what my retirement goals are. ❏

2. I have determined the time frame in which I want to retire. ❏

3. I have looked into the possibility of passing the business on to my heirs. ❏

4. I have considered the possibility of selling the business to an employee. ❏

5. I have looked into the opportunities for selling the business to an outside party. ❏

6. I have assessed the benefits and costs of simply liquidating the company. ❏

7. I have met with my accountant to prepare for the eventual sale of my business. ❏

Chapter
16

What Happens Next?

You've started a business, systematized its operations, and have grown it into a strong, successful, and lucrative company. The business now runs almost by itself with little intervention from you. You frequently entertain unsolicited offers to buy your business, but you're not quite ready to cash out yet. It takes less and less time to manage the business, even as it grows larger. What will you do with your extra time?

To answer that question, you need to go back to examine your personal and business goals, which may have changed over the years as you get a more developed sense of who you are. There are many things you can do with that free time:

- *Relax.* You may decide that you only want to work part time while you pursue hobbies (or those margaritas!).

- *Work in the business.* You may truly enjoy doing what the business does. For example, if you own a law firm, you may really like trying cases. If so, feel free to do that, knowing that you've set up the machine to work on its own.

- *Start another business.* You may choose to go back to the beginning and start up a new business with all of the knowledge and experience you have gained over the years. You now know what it takes to be successful and you can avoid many of the pitfalls that may have snagged you the first time around.

- *Buy and sell businesses.* Another option (if you really enjoyed systematizing and building your business) is to purchase other businesses, fix them up to increase their value, and sell them for a profit. It's sort of like flipping houses. There are many entrepreneurs who have made their fortunes this way.

A Last Word

Owning a successful business has been the dream of entrepreneurs for centuries.

It's as much to do with designing your own destiny and securing your future, as it is to do with the money. It takes a lot of work and planning to create a successful business, but the rewards are certainly worth it. May you always have great happiness and success!

Please feel free to email me at <angie@numbers101.com> to let me know how your business is doing.

Resources for the Growing Business

Online Resources

www.numbers101.com

Our official Web site is packed full of articles, advice, and business tools such as cash flow spreadsheets, templates, and links. You can also sign up for our free newsletter and join our online Numbers 101 community, linking small businesses all over the world.

www.self-counsel.com

Online shopping for a wide variety of business and legal titles (including this one).

www.sba.gov

US Small Business Administration — has lots of great resources for small businesses. Mostly US-focused but useful for businesses in all countries.

www.cfib.ca

Canadian Federation of Independent Business. CFIB is an advocacy group for small businesses. They lobby the government for legislative changes that will assist businesses and their owners. On the website are lease-versus-buy calculators, downloadable publications, and other resources.

http://sme.ic.gc.ca

Performance Plus from Industry Canada. A great website for businesses from all countries. Shows you how your business stacks up with others in your industry.

www.bcentral.com

Microsoft Small Business Resources. Do they want to sell you stuff? Of course! In addition, this website also offers great articles on marketing, promotion, and other business matters.

www.toolkit.cch.com

CCH Business Owner's Toolkit. Great tools and resources including sample business documents, checklists, and government forms.

www.inc.com

The online presence of *Inc. magazine*. Here you will find great articles, tools, and calculators to help your business grow.

Must-Read Books for Entrepreneurs

Building a Shared Vision: A Leader's Guide to Aligning the Organization by C. Patrick Lewis (Oregon: Productivity Press, 1997)

This book helps you to bring your vision down to the organization level.

Good to Great: Why Some Companies Make the Leap and Others Don't by Jim Collins (New York: Harper Business, 2001)

Whether you have one employee or thousands, this book will show you how great leaders make great companies.

Inside the Magic Kingdom: Seven Keys to Disney's Success by Tom Connellan (Bard Press, 1997)

A look at one of the most successful team-oriented companies in the world.

From Worst to First: Behind the Scenes of Continental's Remarkable Comeback by Gordon Bethune (Wiley, 1999).

This book follows Continental's meteoric rise in three years from its mediocre beginnings. A great case study on how strong leadership can make fantastic changes in an organization.

Pour Your Heart Into It: How Starbucks Built A Company One Cup At A Time by Howard Schultz (Hyperion, 1999).

> Starbucks began with the vision of its CEO and the author of this book, Howard Schultz. He has turned it into a marketing phenomenon and one of the fastest growing companies in the world.

Body and Soul by Anita Roddick (Crown Publishing, 1991).

> When Roddick started The Body Shop, she had a very different vision in mind than most entrepreneurs. She shows us that it is possible to succeed by marching to the beat of your own drummer!

The Nordstrom Way: The Inside Story of America's #1 Customer Service Company by Robert Spector & Patrick D. McCarthy (Wiley, 1996).

> Customer service can make or break a company. Learn how Nordstrom has made rabidly loyal customers and how you can too.

McDonald's: Behind the Arches by John F. Love (Bantam, 1995).

> An inside look at the most successful franchise on the planet.

Virgin King: Inside Richard Branson's Business Empire by Tim Jackson (HarperCollins, 1998).

> Richard Branson is one of the most individual and successful entrepreneurs in the world. Learn how he took Virgin Airlines from its humble beginnings to become one of the most-loved and profitable underdogs.

Nuts! Southwest Airlines' Crazy Recipe for Business and Personal Success by Kevin Freiberg and Jackie Freiberg (Broadway Books, 1998).

> There is no other business model quite like Southwest Airlines'. They have truly listened to their customers and have developed fantastic systems to help them meet their goals. A great book on systemization and an in-depth look at a fascinating company.

Glossary

Balance sheet: One of the three major financial statements of a business. (The statement of cash flow and the income statement are the other two.) The balance sheet displays everything of a measurable financial value that is owned and owed by the company.

Budgeting: The process of planning and projecting revenues, expenses, and capital expenditures for future fiscal periods.

Capacity: The upper limit of a company's ability to produce a product or service.

Capital: The resources that a company uses to produce a product or service.

Cash flow: The inflows to and outflows from a business, regardless of the source.

Cash flow statement (also known as the statement of changes in financial position or the statement of cash flows): One of the three major financial statements of a business. (The balance sheet and income statement are the other two.) The cash flow statement, in its most general terms, shows why there is an increase or decrease in cash during the year.

Controller (comptroller): The "big cheese" accountant in an organization. The controller oversees all accounting functions and sometimes operates as the company's chief financial officer.

Conversion rate: The number of potential customers who buy versus the number who inquire about your product or service.

Corporation: One of the three major forms of business ownership (partnership and sole proprietorship are the other two.) A corporation is the only type of business that is legally separate from its owners: it is itself a legal entity. Corporate ownership is shown through the issues of share certificates.

Creditor: A person or other business that has loaned money or extended credit to a company.

Debt: The amounts owed by a business to outside persons or businesses. It is sometimes more narrowly defined as to exclude accounts payable and include only loans that have fixed interest rates and repayment schedules.

Decline: The last of three stages in a company's life cycle, in which revenues and customer base begin to decline. The other two stages are infancy and maturity.

Demand: The desire by consumers for a company's product.

Dividends: The portion of earnings (either current or retained from prior periods) that have been distributed out to the shareholders in the current operating period.

Dun & Bradstreet: A corporate rating agency in the United States.

Earnings: A term usually used interchangeably with net income (i.e., revenues less expenses).

Entrepreneur: A person who envisions and creates a business. This person may or may not be either an investor or manager in the ongoing operations.

Exit strategy: A plan for a company's owners to either sell or wind up the business.

Franchise: A company that designs and builds a business model for entrepreneurs to follow.

General ledger: The grouping of accounts used by a business. Also, the book where the main summary records are kept for each balance sheet and income statement item.

General journal: A detailed record of all financial transactions of a business. The general journal is summarized and entered as net increases and decreases to the accounts in the general ledger.

Goodwill: The value of a business that is not directly attributable to hard assets, but instead to the benefits such as a company's reputation or customer list.

Gross income: Another term for revenues.

Gross margin: Represents revenues minus the cost of goods sold in the period.

Income statement: One of the three major financial statements of a business. (The balance sheet and statement of cash flow are the other two.) The income statement shows operating activity over an operating period from revenues, expenses, and extraordinary gains and losses.

Hard systems: Those business systems that involve tangible procedures (e.g., how a management report is prepared).

Infancy: The first of three stages in a company's life cycle, in which revenues increase exponentially and cash flow is generally strained. The other two are maturity and decline.

Insolvent: A term used to describe a business that does not have enough assets to meet its debt obligations in the short term. Insolvency can lead to bankruptcy if not corrected quickly.

Internal control: Represents the procedures set up in a business to prevent errors and fraudulent activity.

Inventory: Goods held for resale that remain unsold at the end of an operating period. In a manufacturing environment, inventory includes raw materials, goods in the process of being made, and finished goods. In certain service industries, inventory includes time spent on customer activities but not yet billed out.

Life cycle of a business: Represents the three stages of the total existence of a business: infancy, maturity, and decline.

Management operational plan: A company's plan for how it will do business on a day-to-day basis. A management operational plan will include short-term budgets and revenue forecasts as well as analysis of historical performance (see the second book in the *Numbers 101 for Small Business* series, *Financial Management 101* for a more complete discussion of the management operational plan).

Manager: The individual that oversees the production staff and ensures that policies and procedures are being followed.

Market niche: The specific set of consumer demands that are met by a company.

Market share: The ratio of a business's revenue as compared to the revenues of the entire industry.

Maturity: The second of three stages in a company's life cycle, in which revenues and customer base are steady and customer demand has been sated. The other two are infancy and decline.

Mission statement: A company's representation of its vision and how it will achieve it.

Net income: The income left in an accounting period after all expenses have been deducted from revenues. The term net income is used only if the revenues exceed the expenses.

Net loss: The deficit for an accounting period that occurs when the expenses for that period exceed the revenues.

Partnership: One of the three major forms of business ownership (corporation and sole proprietor are the other two). A partnership is an unincorporated business with two or more owners. Partnerships are jointly owned by the partners and do not have a separate "legal life" of their own.

Profit: see **Net income**.

Profit and loss (P&L) statement: Another name for an income statement.

Revenue: The amount of net assets generated by a business as a result of its operations.

Script: A written and rehearsed dialogue for staff members to use when dealing with customers or potential customers to ensure the consistency of the message.

Shareholder: An owner or internal investor of a corporation.

Soft systems: Those business systems that involve intangible procedures, more particularly, the actions of employees (e.g., how a customer is greeted on the telephone, how a customer complaint is handled).

Sole proprietorship: One of the three major forms of business ownership (corporation and partnership are the other two). A sole proprietorship is an unincorporated company owned by a single owner. It has no "legal life" of its own.

Solvency: The ability of a company to settle its liabilities with its assets.

Statement of cash flows: One of the three major financial statements. The statement of cash flow explains the changes in assets, liabilities, and net equity for the period.

Statement of changes in financial position: An older term for the statement of cash flows.

Stockholder: see **Shareholder**.

Systems: The group of business systems that make up the operations of a company.

Turnkey: A business that has had policies and procedures well-documented and tested so that anyone can run it successfully from the very beginning.

Vision statement: A company's overall statement as to how it views itself in the future. A vision statement is broken down further into a measurable mission statement and actionable operational goals.

If you enjoyed this book, get *Financing Your Business: Get a Grip on Finding the Money*, also available from Self-Counsel Press. Here's a preview of its table of contents:

Contents

Introduction

1   So, What Kind of Business Should You Start?
Introduction
Why Do You Want to Be an Entrepreneur?
Money
Freedom
Empire building
What Kind of Business Should I Start?
Manufacturing business
Retail/Wholesale business
Service business
Eight Questions to Ask Yourself

2   Is It a Business or a Hobby?
Introduction

What Is the Difference Between a Business and a Hobby?

It's Not Always about the Money

3   Build or Buy?

Introduction

Building a Business from Scratch

Buying an Existing Business

Financial Considerations in the Build-versus-Buy Decision

    Considering a start-up business

    Considering a business purchase

What's Right for You?

4   Getting Your Personal Finances in Order

Introduction

Your Retirement Goals

    How much will you need at age 60?

    How much do you have to put away between
    now and retirement?

The Concept of Net Wealth

Debt Management

Your Credit History

Insuring Your Assets

    Life insurance

    Mortgage insurance

    Property and casualty insurance

    Health insurance

5   Setting Your Business Goals

Introduction

Chasing the Almighty Buck

What Is the Purpose of Your Business?

The Business Plan

What Should My Business Plan Include?

The Monthly Management Operating Plan

Your Exit Strategy

6 Putting Your Money Where Your Business Plan Is

Introduction

Projecting Your Funding Needs

    Paying for the start-up costs

    Providing liquidity to the business

Sources of Funding

A Bank's Perspective

7 Debt Financing

Introduction

Your Own Resources

Credit Cards

Suppliers

Friends and Family

Banks

Leasing Companies

Private Lenders

8 Equity Financing

Introduction

Common Shares

Preferred Shares

Partnership

Joint Ventures

Venture Capitalists

9 Risky Business: How to Assess Business Risk

Introduction

Secured Loans

Personal Guarantees

Fixed Price Agreements

Interest Rate Risk

Foreign Exchange Risk

Economic Dependence

10 Home Sweet Home

Introduction

Does It Really Save Me Money?

How Will It Affect My Personal Life?

    The neighbors

    The on-call syndrome

    The convenience

    Willpower

11 Choosing Your External Team

Introduction

Your Lawyer

Your Accountant

Your Financial Adviser

Your Board of Directors

12 Assessing the Competition

Introduction

Identify the Competition

What Do They Do Right and Wrong?

How Are They Positioned to Take Advantage
of Opportunities?

How Vulnerable Are They to Changing
Market Conditions?

How Do You Stack Up?

Competitive Analysis

Intelligence Resources

13 Forecasting Profit

Introduction

Keep Your Bookkeeping Up-to-Date

Always Forecast a Rolling 12 Months

Tighten Up Billing and Collection Policies

Hire Someone to Do It If You Can't

Keep on Top of Changes in the Operating Environment

Keep the Work Coming In

Continually Assess New Sources of Financing

14 Investing in Labor

Introduction
The Cost of an Employee
    Salary
    Employer taxes
    Office space
    Fringe benefits
Calculating the Benefit
    Direct labor
    Indirect labor
Your Billing Multiplier
Five Signs It's Time to Hire

15 Investing in Equipment

Introduction
To Buy or Not to Buy
Erosion
Financing
Risk

16 Financing Expansion

Introduction
Horizontal Expansion
    Increase your capacity
    Expand your geographic area
    Develop new products or services
    Develop a franchise
    Find new markets for your existing products
    and services
Vertical Expansion
The Dangers of Expansion
    Liquidity issues
    Triggering call provisions
    Increase in fixed costs
Calculating the Benefits of Expansion
Finding the Money to Expand

Appendix 1

Present Value of $1

Appendix 2

Present Value of an Annuity

Appendix 3

The future Value of an Annuity

Appendix 4

Resources for the Growing Business

Glossary

Samples

1   Cash Flow Projection for a Start-Up Business
2   Discounted Cash Flows for a Start-Up Business
3   Cash Flow Projection for a Business Purchase
4   Discounted Cash Flows for a Business Purchase
5   Business Plan Outline
6   Cash Flow Report
7   Cash Inflows

Tables

1   A Quick Reference to Ratios
2   Equity Statement for a 50/50 Partnership

Worksheets

1   Retirement Planning
2   Competitive Analysis

OTHER TITLES IN THE
SELF-COUNSEL BUSINESS SERIES

Numbers 101 for Small Business

Numbers 101 for Small Business is a series of easy-to-understand guides for small-business owners, covering such topics as bookkeeping, analyzing and tracking financial information, starting a business, growing a business, and exiting a business. Using real-life examples, Angie Mohr teaches small-business owners how to beat the odds and turn their ideas into successful, growing companies.

Bookkeepers' Boot Camp:
Get a Grip on Accounting Basics
ISBN: 1-55180-449-2
$14.95 US / $19.95 CDN

Bookkeepers' Boot Camp teaches you how to sort through the masses of information and paperwork, how to record what is important for your business, and how to grow your business for success!

This book will show you the essentials of record keeping for a small business and why it's necessary to track information. The book will give you a greater understanding of the process of record keeping and a deeper understanding of your business and how it works.

Financial Management 101:
Get a Grip on Your Business Numbers
ISBN: 1-55180-448-4
$14.95 US / $19.95 CDN

This book covers business planning, from understanding financial statements to budgeting for advertising. Angie Mohr's easy-to-understand approach to small-business planning and management ensures that the money coming in is always greater than the money going out!

Financial Management 101 is an in-depth guide on business planning. It's a kick-start course for new entrepreneurs and a wake-up call for small-business owners.

Financing Your Business:
Get a Grip on Finding the Money

ISBN: 1-55180-583-9

$14.95 US / $19.95 CDN

Financing Your Business will show you, in an easy to understand manner, how to raise capital for your small business. Whether you are just starting a new business or you want to expand an existing business, this book helps you to acquire the funds you will need.

Angie Mohr leads you step-by-step through the process and explores all the options available so that you can devise a financial plan that is suited to your company and goals.

ORDER FORM

All prices are subject to change without notice. Books are available in book, department, and stationery stores. If you cannot buy the book through a store, please use this order form. (Please print.)

Name_____

Address_____

Charge to: ❏ Visa   ❏ MasterCard

Account number _____

Validation date _____

Expiry date_____

Signature _____

YES, please send me:

_____ Bookkeepers' Boot Camp

_____ Financial Management 101

_____ Financing Your Business

Please add $4.95 for postage and handling.

Canadian residents, please add 7% gst to your order.

WA residents, please add 7.8% sales tax.

❏ Check here for a free catalog.

IN THE USA

Please send your order to:

Self-Counsel Press Inc.
1704 N. State Street
Bellingham, WA 98225

IN CANADA

Please send your order to the nearest location:

Self-Counsel Press
1481 Charlotte Road
North Vancouver, BC   V7J 1H1

Self-Counsel Press
4 Bram Court
Brampton, ON L6W 3R6

Visit our website at: www.self-counsel.com